MW01156836

GUIDEPOSTS FOR THE SPIRIT:

Stories to Comfort the Soul

Guideposts

FOR THE
Spirit

STORIES TO
COMFORT
THE SOUL

EDITED BY JULIE K. HOGAN

Ideals Publications • Nashville, Tennessee

ISBN 0-8249-4626-X

Published by Ideals Publications
A division of Guideposts
535 Metroplex Drive, Suite 250
Nashville, Tennessee 37211
www.idealsbooks.com

Copyright © 2004 by Ideals Publications

All rights reserved. No part of this publication may be reproduced or transmitted in any
form or by any means, electronic or mechanical, including photocopy, recording, or any
information storage and retrieval system, without permission in writing from the publisher.

Printed and bound in Italy

Library of Congress CIP data on file

Publisher, Patricia A. Pingry
Associate Publisher, Peggy Schaefer
Series Designer, Eve DeGrie
Book Designer, Jenny Eber Hancock
Copy Editors, Melinda Rathjen, Katie Patton
Research Assistant, Mary P. Dunn

Paintings by Sherri Buck Baldwin

10 9 8 7 6 5 4 3 2 1

ACKNOWLEDGMENTS

ALBOM, MITCH. "The Second Tuesday We Talk About Feeling Sorry for Yourself" from *Tuesdays with Morrie*. Copyright © 1997 by Mitch Albom. Used by permission of Doubleday, a division of Random House, Inc. BALDWIN, FAITH. "Blessings in Disguise" from *Many Windows*. Copyright © 1958 by Faith Baldwin Cuthrell. Used by permission of Harold Ober Associates Inc. ELLIS, MEL. "A Gift of Hope" from *The Land, Always the Land*, edited by Ted J. Rulseh. Copyright © 1997 by The Cabin Bookshelf, Mishicot, WI. Used by permission of the publisher. FOX, MICHAEL J. "Summer of Sam" from *Lucky Man*. Copyright © 2002 by Michael J. Fox. Reprinted by permission of Hyperion. FUNICELLO, ANNETTE. "On Compassion and Faith" from *A Dream Is a Wish Your Heart Makes*. Copyright © 1994 by Annette Funicello. Used by permission of Hyperion Books for Children. GIUNTA, RAY. An excerpt from *God at Ground Zero*. Copyright © 2002 by Ray Giunta. Used by permission of Integrity Publishers, Inc. GORDON, ARTHUR. "The Strange Power of Compassion." Used by permission of Mrs. Arthur Gordon. GOSS, BILL. An excerpt from *There's a Flying Squirrel in My Coffee: Overcoming Cancer with the Help of My Pet*. Copyright © 2002 by Bill Goss. Used by permission of Atria Books, a division of Simon & Schuster Adult Publishing Group. GRAHAM, BILLY. "God Promises to Send His Angels" from *Hope for the Troubled Heart*. Copyright ©1991 by Billy Graham. Used by permission of W Publishing, Nashville, TN. HART, CHARLES A. "A Corsage of Purple Flowers" from *Uncommon Fathers*. Published by Woodbine House, Inc. Used by permission of Charles A. Hart. *(Acknowledgments continue on page 256.)*

CONTENTS

Finding Comfort *in* Faith

My flesh and my heart faileth: but God is the strength of my heart, and my portion for ever.
—PSALM 73:26

GOD AT GROUND ZERO

"CHAPLAIN RAY" GIUNTA

It's really important that you know how to handle your stress," I told him. "Your family needs you to be well, and so do your 'brothers' out here. You need to take care of yourself, drink plenty of water, and remember to eat. That will help you deal with the way you feel. It helps me."

Neither of us spoke for a moment. And in the lull, as heavy machinery rolled by us, the pile moved under our feet. It did that a lot during those days. Everyone there came to feel the pile was very much alive with its steam and its heat and its rumbling and groaning. But this movement was like a minor earthquake. It rumbled and shook hard. Most of the time you made sure you were ready for it, but we had been talking so intently that we were both caught by surprise. I looked at him, and he looked at me.

"Wow," I gasped as both of us got our balance again. Then, joking, I added, "Hey, if it falls in, just grab on to my arm, because I'm ready."

He looked puzzled. "What?"

"I mean, I know where I'm going if this thing falls in and takes us with it. I'm going to heaven. I'm ready."

Then he started to laugh. It was one of those hard laughs, a mixture of anger and irony and surprise. He laughed so hard I started to wonder.

"Man, that's amazing!" he finally said. "The message in my life just never seems to change. I played football in high school, in college, and I even played some semi-pro ball. And the one thing every coach I had told me was to be ready. They drilled it—I had to get ready. When I grew up, I got married; I wasn't ready to be a husband. So I had to get ready. When I had a son, I wasn't ready to be a father, so I had to get ready. Now I'm standing here in this place with all this death, and you tell me, I've got to get ready to die?" He shook his head as he steadied his balance on the pile. "Not until right now did I think I needed to get ready to meet my Maker."

"I'm sure you're more ready than you think," I said.

"No, I'm not ready, Father," he said. "I mean, I'm a religious man, I guess, but I don't know about being ready to die."

"Well," I said, "you can get ready. It's real simple. God's taken care of it."

"What do you mean?"

I pointed to the pocket Bible he was still holding inside his big fist. "Being ready isn't being religious. The way your Good Book right there explains it, you're ready if you just believe in the Lord and tell people what you believe. Remember the story about the thief on the cross next to Christ?"

"Yeah. Where is it?"

I turned to the story and showed him. "The thief didn't have time to get ready. He was dying, just like Christ. All he did was acknowledge his need and say he believed who Christ was. And Christ responded by saying that the man would be in paradise with Him that day. So—do you believe?"

"Yeah, I do."

"Okay. You're ready."

The cop stood there a second, staring at me. I could almost see his thoughts churning. Then he pocketed the little Bible, turned, and stepped back to the area he'd been working before we started talking, as if he didn't need me anymore. And perhaps he didn't. Those few minutes were the essential reason for a chaplain to be there, the ministry of presence in its purest form, to leave the hope of God's love with the selfless workers in this horrible place, right when they needed it the most. I caught his eye—he gave me a thumbs-up. And we both went back to the work. Our talk had been one of those special, raw, holy moments offered by a living God big enough to be present in a place reeking of death. It would be a story to inspire and comfort both of us as we faced the grim job of uncovering victims' remains, and a story to cherish in the years ahead.

As I picked up my shovel, I looked at the pile below us, and my heart ached for the victims. I thought about life and death, about anger and peace, about courage and presence. At the very depths of my faith is the need to believe that God was big enough to be there for those who must have waited for death on the floors above and the collapsed ruins below.

And I have to believe that in those stories we will never hear is the truth we cling to—that these innocent people were not only comforted but inspired by a God who was near.

*The only important decision we have to make
is to live with God; He will make the rest.*
—AUTHOR UNKNOWN

WHEN ALL AMERICA GRIEVED

JAMES A. "GENE" THOMAS

The engines ignite and rumble. The blaring roar hits your chest full-throttle as the shuttle rises and clears the tower. As with each and every launch, your heart swells with emotion. Every hope, every dream and prayer, becomes part of the ascent, the slow rush across flawless sky, the beautiful arc of *Challenger*.

I made the final decision to launch the space shuttle *Challenger* on January 28, 1986. As shuttle launch director of NASA's mission 51-L, I'd commanded every aspect of the countdown. The engineers, technicians, and scientists reported to me. The weather updates and vehicle data, every piece of crucial information from across the globe, were passed along to me. It was I, with the aid of hundreds of advisers, who determined the shuttle's readiness to fly.

We had a textbook liftoff at 11:38 A.M., a smooth, slow roll of the vehicle as it rose away from Kennedy Space Center. Proudly I watched as all the team's hard work soared into space with *Challenger* and its crew.

Then, at eleven miles high and nine miles downrange, seventy-three seconds into flight, there was a blast of smoke, followed instantly by a fireball and the rockets shooting away. Something had gone terribly wrong. Desperately, I scanned the sky, hoping to pick out the orbiter circling to land at Kennedy. I told myself

Commander Scobee would have seen disaster coming and separated safely. But I heard the dreaded sound of helicopters rushing out to sea, and my engineer's mind knew what my heart could not accept.

Like everyone in the firing room, I sat in shocked disbelief and prayed the crew had not suffered. I pounded my fist into my hand: *Why? Why, Lord? Why did this happen?* I unclenched my fist. It seemed as if, in an instant, everything had tumbled away into the unknown for me. My belief in the perfectibility of technology, of human endeavor itself, had been shattered.

My voice shook as I called my staff into a conference room. We sequestered ourselves with every inch of videotape, every communication and piece of data. The television monitors played and replayed the explosion, searing it into our consciousness. Scores of those in the control center must have memorized all the film loops and reams of data by the time of the press conference that evening.

With several other colleagues I stood beside Vice President Bush as he reassured the launch team. We watched President Reagan address the nation. "We will never forget them," said the President, "nor the last time we saw them, this morning, as they prepared for their journey and waved good-bye and 'slipped the surly bonds of earth' to 'touch the face of God.'"

We returned to our efforts that night disheartened and completely exhausted. We had worked for hours with no breaks, no food, and few answers. At eleven o'clock that night—having experienced a major setback in everything that had been our life's work, having lost seven dear friends on the shuttle, still waiting to find out what had gone wrong—we decided we could all use some rest and sent everyone home.

As I drove along the empty roads to my house, I retraced all the events of the days leading up to the launch. We'd been plagued by a rash of weather and equipment difficulties. Just that previous night critical sensors and ground hardware had failed. Huge icicles had formed on the launch pad. I had decided to hold the countdown until these problems were solved.

Our launch team and ground support had pushed through a long, hectic night to get the countdown started again. By the time the sun had risen over the Atlantic, the temperature was below freezing, but the air was warming. The weather was perfect for launch, and we stood only three hours behind schedule. I remembered how I'd joked with Commander Scobee and Pilot Smith about launching from Pad B, three miles to the north of the main launch area—as though we could move the whole operation in an instant. The two of them were close friends of mine, and I recalled Scobee's familiar laugh, his agreeing to launch the shuttle from the north pad.

All systems go . . .

Go for main engine start . . .

T minus ten . . .

Nine . . .

At home, I sat in our driveway for such a long time my wife and daughters came out to the car to get me. That night I let go the tears I had held back during the day. I must have cried for an hour in bed for my lost friends. I closed my eyes; still I saw *Challenger*.

The following day, we kept searching for the reason for the accident, as if that would somehow undo it. Everyone at NASA was looking for answers. Had we done something wrong? As the days passed, the more I sought an explanation, the more sorrowful going over the details of the accident became.

At church that next Sunday, I stood to sing the hymns and could only weep. Everyone passed handkerchiefs to me. Still, I found no peace, and later I asked my wife, Juanita, how a person is supposed to cope when it seems the world has been blown apart. "I thought I had everything," I told her. "A wonderful family, a church where I serve as a deacon, an engineering job of my dreams. This shock is unreal to me."

Sitting beside me in the living room, she took my hand. I opened my Bible, which lay on the end table, and turned to Romans. The words leaped out at me, as though I'd been led to them. "For I am persuaded that neither death nor life, nor angels nor principalities nor powers, nor things present nor things to come, nor height nor depth, nor any other created thing, shall be able to separate us from the love of God, which is in Christ Jesus our Lord" (Romans 8:38–39, NKJV).

This was the reminder I needed to have, that nothing can ever keep us apart from God. I held tight to that assurance of his continued grace during those next days and weeks.

I would not have made it through that winter—the constant search for answers, the nation's flags at half-staff, the unrelenting struggle through each new detail—without God and my family. One Sunday early that spring a local pastor asked if I would share my story with his congregation. I agreed because I knew they'd been praying for the families of the crew, as well as for our whole community, which has deep connections to NASA. I felt I owed them an account of what had happened, for they too struggled with the tragedy. At least I could testify to the grace God had shown me. And that day, when I stood before them and began to speak, a vivid memory of the crew came to me.

"We had a barbecue down at the beach," I recalled, "two weeks before launch—two dozen of us around picnic tables piled high with burgers, coleslaw, and cake. We talked and ate into the night, the sound of the surf in the background. I remember Ron McNair showing photos of his kids, the two of us talking about being deacons in our churches. Christa McAuliffe was sitting with her parents, smiling like the schoolteacher you fell in love with in first grade. Dick Scobee seemed supremely confident. Mike Smith was so excited about his first trip into space."

My voice faltered for a moment before I went on.

"We have cookouts like that before every launch," I said. "And, you know, I've never driven home from one of those socials without whispering a prayer for the astronauts."

I went on to describe how the last twenty minutes of the countdown had been orchestrated by computers. At that point, only an engineer's cutoff could have halted the launch. The sun had raised the temperature to thirty-nine degrees. I'd joked with Scobee and Smith on the radio to lighten the mood. Then the launch team leaders reported all systems go . . .

Go for main engine start . . .

T minus ten . . .

Nine . . .

"And when the engines begin to rumble," I told everyone, "you feel it pounding hard in your chest—the sound, the pride, the emotion of it all."

When I finished I looked at the faces of the congregation, and in their eyes I saw the tears I too had shed. Their sorrow was my sorrow. We had suffered this loss together, and talking about it made the tragedy more bearable for all of us.

Hard, factual evidence did eventually come. A real scientific explanation for what had gone wrong: The O-rings, which did not expand in the cold temperature, as well as human and organizational errors, were to blame. For the first time in my life, the solution to a problem was of less significance to me. Healing had come from God to us through one another, not from the factual answers to the questions as to why *Challenger* had exploded.

In the fourteen years since, I have spoken at more than a hundred churches across the country. Every time the realization strikes me with the same potency. So often God reaches out to us through his word and through others—all those people who approach me to tell me exactly where they were when disaster struck that day, seventy-three seconds into *Challenger*'s last flight, and how hearing my story strengthens their faith.

We shared this experience as a nation. It was a turning point in an incredible century, one of those moments when we came face-to-face with our own human frailties and could turn for comfort only to the One who is perfect.

And our hope of you is stedfast, knowing, that as ye are partakers of the sufferings, so shall ye be also of the consolation.

—2 Corinthians 1:7

Our Last Hope

Cathy Gentry

"What a perfect day!" I exclaimed as I lifted seven-month-old Jocelyn from her car seat. Jessica, four, and Jordan, six, scrambled out of our SUV, excited to see Spotted Bear Falls for the first time. My husband, Kirk, five of our guides, and several friends had set out earlier, one mile upriver, on their first fishing trip of the season. The girls and I were arriving to watch as they carried their rafts past the falls that thundered just below.

As owners of the Spotted Bear Ranch for over four years, Kirk and I had hosted hundreds of guests who came to the northwestern Montana wilderness. Though being a mother was my first priority, I still felt a personal responsibility to ensure that all our clients have the best time possible. Each morning I put out a prayerful request for sunshine, wanting every one of our guests to remember a picture-perfect stay.

I wanted golden days for my family too, and the kids were clearly enjoying this one. The sun darted through the towering pine trees, scattering patches of light across the forest floor. Always our little free spirit, Jessica was the first to bound down the path. "Come on, Mommy!" she called, singing as she ran toward the river.

Our newest guide, Matt, joined Jessica on the narrow trail that zigzagged down the mountain through blue lupine and sweet wild roses. I could see Kirk and the others carrying rafts to the river several hundred yards below.

"Hey, girlies!" Our guide Dave waved to us, balancing the end of a raft on his head. The girls giggled and waved back. Dave had worked for us for three years and had won my daughters' hearts with his tender roughhousing and goofy jokes.

By the time we reached the riverbank the rafters were putting their equipment in the water to continue their trip. Record snowfalls that winter and an unseasonably warm spring had combined to create a torrent of white, frothing rapids and dark, swirling depths.

"Don't even think about going near the river!" I cautioned my little girls, waving them back about twenty feet. As the girls dug in the sand, I sat with the baby, watching the water thunder past a bend one hundred feet downstream, where the guides were loading the last of the equipment onto the rafts.

After about ten minutes, Kirk waved that the fishing party was ready to go. "Come on, Jessica and Jordan," I said, standing up with the baby. "Time to tell everyone good-bye. Wash your hands in that puddle." I gestured toward one of the water-filled cavities in the rocks close to us.

"Okay, Mom," said Jordan. I turned to see what Jessica was up to. She was nowhere to be seen.

I looked around. "Jessica?" To my horror I saw her standing in a pool at the edge of the river, knee-deep in dark-green water. "Jessica!" I screamed above the roar of the falls. Still clutching the baby in one arm, I ran toward my four-year-old.

"Mom!" She was trying to get a foothold on the slick moss. I headed across a boulder at the water's edge, stretching out my arm—but she slid backward. Her mouth opened, but before she was able to scream Jessica was sucked into a swirling whirlpool.

My feet skidded on the slick surface. I sat down hard, sliding helplessly into the same churning water that had swallowed Jessica. I lifted the baby above my head as the icy water covered my legs, my waist, then my shoulders. As if in slow motion, the cold river closed over my head.

A strong arm circled my waist; I felt someone pulling me up. Matt, hearing my screams, had come running and plunged into the whirlpool after us. With one hand, he managed to cling to the boulder. With the other, he held my baby and me.

Kirk and several of the men had rushed to the boulder above us and were able to hoist the baby out. "Jessica's in here too!" I screamed. "She's been sucked under!"

It took three men to pull Matt and me out of the swirling vortex. Nearly two minutes had passed with no sign of Jessica. I fell to my knees. "God, Jessica loves you and you love her," I prayed. "Be with her. Please save her."

Within seconds there was a shout: "There she is!" Some thirty feet away Jessica's body had shot up out of the water, literally spit out by the whirlpool. Floating face-down in the swift current, she spun to the center of the river. As the rushing water carried her along, the men raced over the rocks and stationed themselves at different points downstream.

"Grab her!" Another guide plunged into the river and seemed poised to catch her, but a surge of water sent her somersaulting past him like a rag doll. A friend lunged into the water but could not jump far enough out to catch her, and she spun past him.

Only one person remained between our daughter and the bend of the river, where Jessica would be lost to us forever. Dave had been running along the bank, trying to stay ahead of her, and now he strode forcefully into the raging torrent until he was chin-deep. A former college football player who stood six foot four, Dave planted himself in Jessica's path, then opened his arms and waited as Jessica's tiny body whirled toward him. As her pale form disappeared beneath the foam, he reached out. Shouts went up. "He's got her!"

As Dave struggled to the bank, Kirk met him halfway out, taking Jessica's limp body and carrying her to shore.

"Let them work on her," someone said, trying to hold me back. "They know what they're doing." No one wanted me to see the results of the river's devastation. Jessica's face was blue, her lips purple, her eyes open in an empty stare and her chest bloated with water. Chris, one of our longtime guides, began CPR.

As the moments passed, Jessica lay unmoving, as lifeless as the gray river rocks. How had this golden day turned so tragic? I was shocked, shivering, horrified. And yet as Chris continued to work on my little girl, peace flowed around me, more solid than the boulders, more powerful than the unstoppable river: Whatever happens, Jessica will be with God. Whatever happens. "Breathe, honey," I whispered, taking deep breaths myself, as if to will her lungs to respond.

There was a weak cough, then a sputter. Jessica sucked in air, coughed again—and started to breathe! Kirk gathered her in his arms and we dashed up the steep mountainside, knowing she was not yet out of danger. By the time we had driven her to the ranger station eight and a half miles away, Jessica had said a few words. She waved from the helicopter as she and Kirk were flown to Kalispell Regional Hospital.

The doctors released Jessica that evening, and our family returned to the ranch to embrace the heroes who had saved her. Later I realized I had been released as well—from the pressure of trying to make all my days, everyone's days, picture-perfect. I had learned that life can be as unpredictable as pools of water along the Spotted Bear River. On the most golden days, events may occur that no one can foresee. But even in unexpected tumult, God's strength and strong arms will always be there to comfort us.

*Be careful for nothing; but in every thing by prayer
and supplication with thanksgiving let your requests
be made known unto God.*

—PHILIPPIANS 4:6

ON COMPASSION AND FAITH

ANNETTE FUNICELLO

Although I generally felt fine, through 1991 it was getting harder to deny that something was wrong. For a few days I was overcome with what felt like a bad case of flu, complete with chills and a fever so dangerously high that I had to lie in bed on packs of ice. Because I have multiple sclerosis, and viral infections are known to exacerbate symptoms, I found myself suddenly unable to walk. If Glen weren't there to carry me, I had to maneuver myself onto the floor and crawl to the bathroom. It was terrifying, yet after a few days the symptoms disappeared.

Just learning that you have MS is such a devastating shock that you sometimes think nothing else could shake you like that again. But to have any chronic illness is to experience a constant series of frightening surprises, some annoying, others almost emotionally devastating. For me the bout of flu really drove home what this MS thing was all about. Even though I had occasionally needed a cane to walk, until then I still thought nothing truly awful could ever happen to me. I guess you could say I almost started to believe my own press. . . .

I don't recall exactly what day it was, but I knew the supermarket tabloids would be out on Friday, and I was sure there would be some story about me, true or not. The only thing to do was to tell the story myself. . . .

Thursday on the front page of *USA Today*'s "Life" section ran the headline "Funicello Fighting Multiple Sclerosis." That morning I read and reread the story, feeling so exposed, yet so relieved. I could go anywhere now and never have to lie again. Nor would my kids, or Glen, or anyone else I cared for. To finally be free just to talk about it after all those years—I can't even explain what that meant.

Then the doorbell rang. Then the phone rang. And before the day was over I'd received dozens of floral arrangements and talked to people I never thought I'd hear from again. And so it continued for several weeks afterward. I received lovely flowers from Frank Sinatra. . . . I had a warm conversation with Paul Anka. . . . And, of course, Frankie let me know he and his wife, Kay, were there for me as well.

I was deeply touched by the thousands of cards and letters, all expressing warm wishes and many containing tips on dealing with MS. And the flowers! Some mornings I'd wake up and walk from room to room, amazed that these were all meant for me, that so many people cared so much. At the same time, though, I also felt a glimmer of panic. *What have I done now?* I thought to myself. *How can I ever thank everyone for their support?* . . .

The first time I went out in public and no one asked me what was wrong, I knew I'd done the right thing. Going public also gave me countless opportunities to talk about MS and to heighten public awareness about this baffling illness. For me, though, the most valuable aspect of being known as a person with MS is getting to meet others who either have it or care for someone who has it. . . .

Glen, God bless him, reads every piece of mail that comes our way. He talks to people who claim they've had success treating people with MS, and he's flown all over the country searching for my answer. But so far the trail's come up cold. That's not to say that there aren't people out there with MS who have had some relief from their symptoms, or what appears for now to be a total remission. But nearly three-quarters of all MS patients experience a spontaneous remission, making it virtually impossible for anyone to pinpoint exactly the cause or evaluate the effectiveness of any given treatment. . . .

Over the past seven years I believe that I've come to terms with MS. It's a part of my life that I could certainly do without, that I would give up joyously if I had the chance. Have I accepted it? Well, it depends on what you mean. Am I happy I have it? Of course not; no one is. But the difference between my attitude now as compared to several years ago is that while I fight the illness every way I can, I no longer fight the realization that I have it. This is not to say that I've given up hope; I certainly have not and never will. But I've stopped expending valuable energy on the "why" of it all—I'll never know why—and instead I focus on what's good about each day, whether it be something as simple as a hug from one of my kids or as grand as a public award. Or, as I used to sing about fifty years ago, I *ac-cent-tchu-ate* the positive. It works. . . .

Until last year I did very well walking with a cane. I've collected quite a number of them, including one of clear Lucite that the Disney artists decorated with characters. But last spring I noticed it was getting harder to find my balance. One day I started to fall and missed toppling face first into a glass tabletop by mere inches. I started using a walker on those more difficult days, and that summer, after trying hard to avoid it, I allowed myself to be seen in public in a wheelchair. Glen and I were at the airport, and our gate was the farthest from the main terminal. I knew I wasn't going to make it. Yet it was hard to ask for it. For me, as for many people, the wheelchair symbolizes disability in a way a cane does not. It marks another step in the progression of the illness, something no one likes to think about.

But as Glen pushed the chair through the terminal, people stopped, grabbed my hand, kissed me, and pinched my cheeks. "God bless you, Annette."

"I grew up with you, Annette, and I'm praying for you."

"You'll get better; I know it."

By the time we reached our gate, I was crying, partially from joy, seeing how deeply people cared, and partially from the frightening realization that one day I may be in a wheelchair more often than I'd like.

Through it all the one constant in my life has been faith. My faith in God is such that I believe that my illness has a purpose and a meaning, although I would never presume to imagine what that might be. Yet, as I build my research foundation, as I travel across the country speaking about MS and my experience, perhaps I can offer others comfort and hope. Perhaps for now that is enough.

The Lord has been good to me throughout my life; He's never let me down. Perhaps this is His test for me. Perhaps it is His way to teach me something I might not have otherwise learned. Whatever it is, I feel the Lord at my side, and with Him I know that all good things are possible.

On Easter Sunday 1993 I believe I felt Him especially close to me. My whole family had gathered for the weekend, and that morning I woke up and walked as easily as ever. It was as if the MS had suddenly vanished. My legs felt light, and my balance was perfect. For that whole day I never needed my cane, I never teetered for a second. It seemed like a miracle. And yet the next day the symptoms returned. Now I pray that one day like that will come again, and then another and another.

I have a recurring dream that one day I rise from a chair and start walking. I can hear my kids saying, "Mom, look at you! You don't even have your cane!" And then I stop and realize that I really am walking again.

"You're right!" I say in the dream. "I am walking!" And someday that dream, that wish, may come true.

I have set before you life and death, blessing and cursing: therefore choose life.
—DEUTERONOMY 30:19B

EPIPHANY AMONG THE LILIES

KATHLEEN TREANOR WITH CANDY CHAND

Kathleen Treanor lost three family members in the 1995 Oklahoma City bombing of the Murrah Building: her mother-in-law and her father-in-law, and her four-year-old daughter, Ashley.

How I longed for my daughter to pick the flowers today, to watch the soft petals caress her face. I knelt down in the grass, overcome with the sense of her presence. Seeing her flowers in full bloom was like receiving a hug from heaven.

I was suddenly overwhelmed with my need to hold her just once more. My tears fell on the petals, then slid to the soil. I looked up to the heavens. "*Oh, God,*" I cried, "how could you let them take my precious daughter from me? I just need to understand. What did I do to deserve this pain? Why am I being punished so harshly?" I collapsed onto the ground and lay there sobbing uncontrollably. "Why? Why? Why?" I wailed.

As my heart continued to break, words of comfort came softly. "Don't you remember, Kathleen? I also lost my child. Like yours, he suffered a cruel, needless death. I know your pain. I did not cause it. But I gave all my children the choice to love and obey me. This is the price of their disobedience."

"But, God," I pleaded, "I'd returned in faith. I was setting my life on the right path. I don't understand. Why are you punishing me now?"

"My child, I am not punishing you. Others have caused your heartbreak. It was their choice, and they chose death."

"But you were supposed to protect me from this. Why did you let this happen to me?"

Everything was beginning to make sense. God had been trying to protect me from pain, but I wouldn't listen. I had refused to heed His repeated warnings. He had known all along what was going to happen and had tried to prepare me, to protect me from harm.

I sighed heavily. "What am I supposed to do with this wisdom now, God? It's too late for me to go back and change anything."

"Be patient. Everything will unfold before you, and in time you'll understand. But first, you must begin to live."

I gazed at Ashley's flowers. They seemed to be radiating from within, almost pulsating with the spirit of my daughter. My eyes swept the perimeter of my yard. In that moment I had a clear, newfound understanding and sense of inevitability. . . . I needed to put myself back together—for them. My family was relying on me to get through this. I had a responsibility to set a good example, to learn to live again.

On a larger scope there were countless people around the world who'd been touched by Ashley's story. Didn't I need to share my faith with them, to show how God can bring His people through times of trouble? This was the very opportunity I'd asked for. Surely my prayers had been answered. I'd been given a powerful message. I wanted God to use me. All I needed to do now was pull myself together, to lean on faith for strength and begin to live.

I knew it wouldn't be easy. There were still unanswered questions and many steps to take. I had much to learn, and more wounds to heal. As I looked at the monumental task before me, I wondered what the future would hold. Then I quietly shook off my concerns. *Trust in God,* I thought. *Take each day, just one step at a time.*

A verse from the Bible came to mind. Although I'd memorized it in my childhood, at that moment the words offered fresh comfort: "To appoint unto them that mourn in Zion, to give unto them beauty for ashes, the oil of joy for mourning, the garment of praise for the spirit of heaviness; that they might be called trees of righteousness, the planting of the LORD, that He might be glorified" (Isaiah 61:3).

Suddenly images from a dream raced through my mind. Only this time, instead of panic, I was offered fresh understanding. A sense of peace and purpose enveloped my being. Perhaps the dream was not a cruel reminder of my loss after all but instead God's comfort, Ashley's comfort, attempting to lift from my presence the dark, unspeakable grief. My daughter had gone to heaven, and no matter how hard I chased her it wasn't time for me to go. Ashley was waiting for me, but for now my place was on earth. I knew then, my dream was a metaphor for the way I'd been living. I'd been chasing her for so very long.

What about Ashley's question only a few days before the bombing? Would I be sad if she died? My natural instinct had been to shudder at the unthinkable, to tell her I'd miss my little girl terribly. Yet in her innocence she'd offered words of comfort. Ashley had reminded me she'd be in heaven with Jesus, that she'd be an angel watching over me.

Suddenly it all made sense. I couldn't change what had happened, but I could continue the mission which Ashley's short life had set me upon. She had a new home now, and for this moment in time I couldn't join her. I knew she was in heaven, and

I would see her again one day—she told me so in my dreams.

I got up, wiped the tears from my eyes, brushed the grass from my body, and began to move about the yard. My pink climbing roses were in full bloom, and the air was filled with their sweet fragrance. I caressed their delicate petals and inspected the trellises. They were sorely in need of attention.

I went to the garden shed, took out my tools, and got to work. I removed the weeds and began pulling up bulbs. The daffodils needed tending. I replanted the iris. Throughout the day I worked, moving daylilies from the back of the house to the front, lining the porch. I set a border around the lilac bush and cleaned out the weeds beneath it. I trimmed the dead limbs from the climbing roses and tied the branches to their trellis.

As Michael came down the drive from work, I looked up. I must have been a sight. He approached me with a knowing smile as he brushed the dirt from the bridge of my nose. "Well, it's about time you joined the living. What have you been up to all day?"

"I've been communing with nature. I really missed you," I said, as I hugged him around the neck. Michael gently pulled away, then looked at me closely, trying to read between the lines. "Are you okay?"

I shrugged. "I hope you're not tired. We have a deck to finish."

Michael smiled broadly. "Give me just a minute." He went into the house just long enough to get a cup of coffee and change into a T-shirt. When he returned I was waiting with hammer and wrecking bar in hand.

We went to work tearing out the old deck. It had rotted in many places and needed to be replaced. We worked side by side, and planned the renovation as we went. When we came to a place where Michael didn't understand what I wanted, we'd stop, sit down, and talk.

I didn't tell him what had happened to me that morning. I was still trying to understand it myself. Instead, I drew strength from his quiet presence and gentle enthusiasm. We worked hard until dark, together once again. It was the first time since the bombing I had not spent the entire day crying. The hard work had other benefits too—I was exhausted. That night I rested soundly, not relying on my prescription drugs to fall asleep. As I slipped into blissful oblivion, I knew change was in store.

On that beautiful spring morning, God reached deep into my soul and performed a miracle. Although He'd been patiently waiting, guiding, and offering comfort all along, I hadn't always felt His presence. I understood this healing was not dependent on my own strength, or even the strength of my family, but on God alone. It was His strength that enabled me to cope. He'd spoken to my heart and given me reasons to go on, to walk out of the darkness and into the light. He understood, had been where no one else could go, saw the depths of my heart's cry, the inner workings of my soul. He quietly offered His extended hand, a way out of my torment. I had only to reach out and accept the help I so desperately needed.

I knew then as I know now—in Him is strength, joy, life, and purpose. The decision was up to me. With a thankful heart I reached out and took His hand. I chose God. I chose my family. I chose to live.

The principal part of faith is patience.
—GEORGE MACDONALD

HAPPY AGAIN

CONSTANCE KIRK

Sunshine burst through the tall glass windows and the first light notes of the "Appalachia Waltz" sounded from the string trio. I took a deep breath, squeezed my bridal bouquet of white calla lilies, and started my slow procession down the aisle. How happy I felt in this moment, happier than I'd ever dreamed possible. Ken, my groom, took my arm and we approached the altar. My best friend stood beside me as my honor attendant. Her bouquet of pink calla lilies was perfect, the sturdy, cylindrical petals peeking out from a spray of baby's breath. *Like spongy pink hair curlers,* I thought. Hair curlers. Not the most romantic comparison, but one that had special significance to me. In a way it was curlers that had gotten me here today.

Seven years ago, I'd taken a short trip to New York City. It had been ages since I'd spent the night alone in a hotel. Just divorced at thirty-four, I'd forgotten how to enjoy anything on my own. A favorite restaurant, an afternoon movie, even the church my husband and I had attended every Sunday all seemed strange without him, and I ended up staying at home more and more. I lay on top of the thin hotel bedspread, staring up at the stucco ceiling. *Will I ever get used to this?*

I woke up in the same position at 3:00 A.M. The hotel fire alarm was going off. Quick as I could I pulled on a robe, grabbed my room key, and joined the other guests filing into the parking lot. I stared at the ground, running a bare toe over the gravel while firemen checked out the problem. A flash of pink caught my eye, and I stepped forward to see what it was. The crowd parted around me to reveal a little lady in a ter-rycloth bathrobe and slippers. Her gray hair was completely rolled in dozens of pale-pink curlers, and she held her robe tight to her neck. *She's all alone, like me,* I thought. *I wonder if she's scared.* I stood beside her, as much for her comfort as for mine.

"What brings you here?" the woman turned and asked.

I looked into her face. She seemed to be in her seventies, but her twinkling eyes belied her age. "I needed to get away," I said. "I recently divorced, and the future seems so uncertain." Had I just said that to a complete stranger?

The woman put her hand on my arm and shook her head, making the curlers bounce. "Oh, you mustn't think like that," she said. She leaned in close. I bent down to listen, bumping my nose on a spongy pink curler. "Keep the faith," she whispered in my ear. "The best is yet to come." Could that really be true? Looking into the woman's sparkling eyes, I couldn't help but think that maybe, just maybe, it could be.

"False alarm," the hotel manager called out. "We apologize for the inconvenience." I held out my arm to escort the woman back into the hotel, but she was no longer standing beside me. I scanned the crowd for the head full of pink curlers. *Strange*, I thought. Not just her disappearance, but the warm, hopeful feeling in my chest.

I took the feeling back home with me, determined to make a new life for myself. The first time I entered a restaurant alone I wanted to run right out the door before I even looked at the menu. I forced myself to stay. And traveling filled me with dread no matter where I was going. "This just isn't working," I sighed one evening after returning home early from a weekend at the beach. "I just can't hack it alone." But before I could throw out my suitcases, I heard the voice of the lady in pink curlers: "Keep the faith. The best is yet to come."

Keep the faith. Had I really been doing that? I hadn't been to church since my divorce. *It's time to give it a try,* I decided. After all, there were other churches in New

York besides the one I'd belonged to with my husband. I just had to find the one that was right for me.

I started visiting, and my prayer was the same in each church: "God, I need your help finding my place in this world." It wasn't easy sitting in a pew by myself, but it wasn't impossible, either. Each Sunday was a small victory. I began to venture out on my own: movies, museums, bookshops. Eventually I decided to use my frequent flyer miles and take a weeklong solo trip to Paris. *The best is yet to come,* I reminded myself on the Champs-Elysées.

Upon my return, I resumed my Sunday research. I'd visited a dozen churches before I finally dropped in at St. Clement's, which I'd often walked past. The building left a lot to be desired, its red paint peeling, but I got a good feeling as soon as I sat down inside. The preacher had a way of speaking that drew me in and made me feel right at home. "Loving God is a process," he said. "It brings us out of isolation and into the embrace of a community."

I went back to St. Clement's the following Sunday, and the next after that. In between I actually enjoyed my life, even the quiet times alone. In fact, I found myself scheduling time alone. I was happy again. Soon I wasn't waiting for Sunday to go to church. I volunteered for some of the outreach programs the church sponsored and got to know the preacher. We became quite good friends along the way. That friendship turned to love, and Ken asked me to marry him. I'd never been so sure of anything as I was about accepting his proposal.

The final notes of the string trio faded, and I turned to face Ken for our vows. I looked into his eyes as he slipped the wedding ring on my finger and thought about that little lady in the hotel parking lot, pink curlers bobbing in her hair. "The best is yet to come," she'd said and she was right. I had found happiness, on my own and with Ken. All I had to do was keep the faith. A faith that today Ken and I keep together.

Thou wilt keep him in perfect peace,
whose mind is stayed on thee: because he trusteth in thee.
—Isaiah 26:3

THE GIFT OF ADVERSITY

Ruth Stafford Peale

At is difficult for me to forget one of the most frightening experiences of my life. Norman and I had just come home from a full Sunday of church and friends and shopping. We were still laughing and enjoying the day when we walked into our living room in New York City and found a message to call a surgeon at the University of North Carolina Hospital in Chapel Hill. My heart sank.

Our son, John, had been completing his studies for a doctorate at the university there. Norman picked up the phone to return the call, and I stood next to him, anxious and waiting. When Norman reached the surgeon, he held the phone between us so I could also hear what he was saying.

"Your son came into the emergency room of the hospital today. He was in agony. So we tested him throughout the afternoon and we've arrived at the diagnosis of inflamed gallbladder with probable pancreatic complications." I took a deep breath as he continued. "We're medicating him, trying to delay operating because it's too dangerous with a gallbladder in this condition. We hope to reduce the infection and bring down his temperature first, and then operate on him later.

"Well, Doctor," I whispered, "John is in your hands and he is in God's hands. You do what you think is best." When Norman thanked him and hung up the phone, we went immediately into prayer: praying for the doctor, praying for our only son, and asking God to help us through this time.

At 11:15 that night, the doctor called back to tell us that John had not responded to medication. The situation was becoming very serious, and he did not like operating under such conditions. Again, he felt it was too dangerous for surgery. "But it might be more dangerous not to," he said. "I think I'm going to have to operate."

Then I heard myself repeat to him, "Doctor, he is in your hands and in God's hands. Dr. Peale and I will be with you in prayer. Bring him through this for us."

"I'll try mighty hard," he told us. Norman and I then faced each other and realized we ran the risk of losing our only son. We knew he was in great danger, but all of our lives we had tried to practice the idea of letting go and letting God be in control of the situation. Still, it is never easy to let go of your own son when everything within you draws him to you. We prayed again and asked God for his help in achieving this.

The doctor had said he would call us back in about two to three hours, when the operation was over. But he did not call us back. Six hours went by. We literally prayed all night long and waited for the phone to ring. Even though no word had come from the surgeon, at about 3:30 A.M., I had a strong conviction that it was somehow going to be all right with John and that I could leave him in the hands of God. I told this to Norman. He looked me in the eye and said, "Ruth, I had the same feeling a few moments ago."

By six o'clock that morning, the doctor finally called us. I picked up the phone and heard him say, "Mrs. Peale, I'm glad to report that John came through the operation successfully. He's very sick but he's also a healthy young man. He's lived a clean life and that counts when the chips are down. I think he's going to be all right."

It had been a long time since I had experienced the overwhelming sense of the greatness and love of God I experienced that morning. Later I learned that at about

3:00 A.M., the situation had become so serious that they brought the hospital's chief surgeon in to take part in John's operation. And when I told the doctor that I had been praying for my son all night, he said, "I always try to work in partnership with God!"

Certainly every family has its share of emergencies and difficult times. For us, John's surgery was a crisis that I have to admit frightened me a great deal. The thought of nearly losing our only son was a test I wouldn't wish on anyone. Though at first I was worried, all I could think to do was pray. And when we finally received the doctor's call, I suddenly had a renewed sense of God's faithfulness and mercy. In other words, what others might have called a great adversity, I saw as a gift.

Throughout our lives, all of us experience times of trial, challenge, or conflict, and how we choose to confront them very often can make a world of difference. For instance, if I had given up on John and just worried all night long, I would have become bitter, and probably made Norman miserable as well. But learning to give my concerns over to God helped me to remember who's really in control. That is why I believe we can learn a great deal about living positively through the gift of adversities.

I am not suggesting that we go looking for hard times or painful challenges. If we wait a little while, they'll come. No, I think we need to exercise wisdom in all we do. I don't know any person who has not had some level of trouble come their way, most of the time because of circumstances they had absolutely no part in. The bottom line is simply that life can and does hand us its share of hardships, yet how we choose to deal with them can make all the difference. I have come to believe that instead of running from difficulties or trying to pretend they aren't there, we need to see them as opportunities that we can learn from. When we do, we begin to reshape our attitudes and get the most out of life.

No winter lasts forever; no spring skips its turn.
—HAL BORLAND

A GIFT OF HOPE

MEL ELLIS

Borgese (there must have been more to his name though I never heard it) was a great (or was it a great-great?) uncle. I was very young and he always arrived without warning and at rare intervals. With him came romantic stories of Alaskan goldfields, tropical seas, windswept deserts and craggy mountains, exotic tales of faraway places. An angular man with cut-stone features that seemed ageless, he did magical things with a deck of cards, a silver dollar, a silken handkerchief, an apple, a walnut, even my own jackknife, which time and again mysteriously left my pocket for his. No matter the season or the familial mood, he brought sunshine into our home during his regulation two-day stays, after which he would pick up what he called his ditty bag and head down the street for the railroad depot.

Then there was the final visit. It was October, and already mornings were bitterly cold, World War I had ended nearly a year ago. With the country well into the postwar depression, the once-a-week pint of Sunday ice cream had been scratched from the grocery list, and we were looking toward many wintertime meals of fried dough made palatable with wild plum jam, currant jelly or sauce from the apple slices drying in the attic.

That October, Borgese did not come jauntily walking up the road, but came seated beside the driver of the dray wagon that delivered goods from the railroad depot to the dry goods store, the funeral and furniture parlor, and the old yellow brick hotel. What is more, he did not have his ditty bag, but a black teakwood steamer trunk, bound sturdily in brass, with a lock the size of a dog collar dangling from a sturdy iron hasp. It took much grunting and groaning from both Borgese and the drayman to get the chest onto the porch. Instead of his usual gusty, "Say there mates, how've we all been?" he smiled, I thought sadly, and said instead, "Well, now, hello." That evening, as soon as he and Dad had wrestled the trunk up the winding staircase to the attic, he went to the spare room. Then, when mother knocked to say supper was ready, he said through the closed door, "You just all go ahead. I'm not hungry tonight."

Next morning, when he failed to answer my knock, I dared open the door an inch to peek in. His head, on the pillow with eyes closed, was as blue-white as carved marble. Dad was summoned from work. He opened the envelope on the washstand. There was money and an address to which his body was to be shipped, and in another envelope on the bureau was the key to the steamer trunk, along with instructions not to open it until the following May 1. . . .

As we had anticipated, and as the *Farmer's Almanac* had predicted, it was a cold, ice-hard, frightening winter, with frost sometimes creeping nearly a foot along the floor from beneath all except the kitchen door where the cooking range roared until it was a blistering red. In retrospect, it was the kind of winter that might have splintered family solidarity, a winter of bickering and backbiting, a winter such as might have sent a lesser father packing, a lesser mother to bed with any of a dozen convenient ailments, a winter that might have turned a clutch of caring kids into a rebellious, hate-filled gang.

But remember, there was the brassbound teakwood trunk. At first, none spoke of it, though each, finding a chance, crept into the icy attic to see if the trunk was still there, to touch it and sit on it, wondering what manner of treasures might be locked inside. Christmas came with a snarl of wind, turning what might have been a beautiful fall of snow into a raging blizzard. There was an orange for each, a small bag of hard candy, mittens for all, a tablet and pencil for each child, and popcorn to be eaten when it came off the small spruce Christmas tree destined to become fuel for the kitchen range.

Bleak might have been the word to describe that Christmas, except for the steamer trunk, which we had bounced down the attic steps to a place of honor beside the tree. Then, when the tree candles were lit, the trunk, its brass rubbed to a high gold finish, the dark brown teakwood rubbed with lard until it appeared to have been varnished, was our star of Bethlehem, the treasure at the rainbow's end, all the gifts of the Magi kept preciously secret and secure by the enormous lock that sometimes seemed to scream: "Do not open until May!"

The trunk never got back to the attic. It found a place where any in the house would have to walk around it a dozen times a day. Magically, frozen fingers ceased to pain. Chilblains hardly itched at all. The absence of meat on the table was no big thing. And no matter how weary or cold, all on arriving home looked each time to make sure the trunk was still there before hurrying to the kitchen's comforting warmth. Magically, too, the days seemed to speed down the weeks of each month as the sun rose earlier and set later. Even business began to pick up. I got a part-time job, as did one other in that clutch of kids. There were checkers and cards and good talk and laughing in the kitchen before bedtime. And always there was the trunk, filled with mysterious promise.

Of course, no one thought of going to bed when April 30 arrived. It was unusually warm, and after dark we drifted quietly in and out of the house to count the stars and watch the clock. Before the clock began to strike, we all had gathered around. As the clock struck the final second away for all time, father inserted the huge key, the lock grated, and we all waited breathlessly as the heavy lid lifted and the trunk creaked open.

As one, we leaned forward, and it seemed like forever before Father said: "Nothing. There's nothing. Nothing except stones."

Mother bent closer and reached down. "There's an envelope."

She handed it to Father, and his hand shook while opening it to bring out a single sheet of paper. Father read it, then handed it to Mother. I leaned closer to see her face more clearly. A tiny smile was starting to curl the corners of her lips. Then she read, "Many happy springtimes!"

"That's all?" we asked, almost in unison.

"That's all," Mother said.

Stunned, we went to bed. And yet, we felt no residual resentment or grief the next morning, because all the sweet smells of spring were coming through the open windows. Brothers were laughing about the great joke Borgese had played on us, and how typical it was of him. It was not until many years later that I realized that Borgese had intended this, and I could appreciate how hope moves any through a winter or a life to many happy springtimes.

We must accept finite disappointment,
but we must never lose infinite hope.
—MARTIN LUTHER KING JR.

THE LIGHTHOUSE

CHRISTOPHER REEVE

Not long ago I wrote an essay about hope. It's a story about surviving an almost impossible situation; perhaps it's also the best way I can describe how I feel about my new life.

I have always loved sailing. I loved being out on the water, in harmony with the boat, feeling the exhilaration of slicing through waves, leaving land behind. The most precious moments were shared with friends, working together to bring out the best in the boat and in ourselves.

In the late fall of 1978, I helped deliver a forty-eight-foot sloop from Connecticut to Bermuda. There were five of us onboard for the journey down the Connecticut River, eastward on Long Island Sound around the point at Montauk, then due south in search of a tiny island 564 miles off the Carolinas. We expected a passage of four to five days.

Casting off just before midnight, we caught the ebb tide that would push us quickly downriver and out into the Sound. With a bracing fifteen-knot breeze behind us, we sped past the houses on the shoreline and watched them go dark as people settled into their cozy beds. We had on thermals, sweaters, and foul weather gear to protect us against the thirty-eight degree October night. Clutching our mugs of coffee, ducking now and then to avoid the stinging spray from the bow wave, we embraced the adventure ahead.

By daybreak we had rounded Long Island and Montauk lay astern. As it disappeared over the horizon we knew we would not see land again for the next four days. The wind shifted to the west and picked up to twenty knots; the boat was "in the groove" as we sped southward at nearly fifteen miles an hour. We shifted into the routine of offshore sailing, each of us on watch for four hours then off the next four. All of us were experienced sailors but we hadn't met before the trip. Three were from England, one was a Canadian friend of the owner who lived in Toronto, and I was the American.

The next two days passed quickly as we enjoyed good weather, took turns preparing reasonably appetizing meals, and started to get acquainted. Although the boat was equipped with radar and the most advanced electronic navigation system of its time, we still tracked our progress as sailors have for centuries—with a sextant and dead reckoning. Every few hours we tuned in to the weather reports on the high frequency radio. On the afternoon of the third day, we didn't like what we heard.

The storm came from the north and reached us just before dark. We were sailing directly downwind with the mainsail and jib full out at right angles to the boat. The rain came first, then the following seas rose until they towered above us. Suddenly the wind gusted to thirty and thirty-five knots; all hands came on deck to take down the jib and put two reefs in the main. Even with the reduced sail area, we were now sledding down mountainous waves, the bow crashing into the troughs below as the storm turned into a full-blown gale.

We couldn't see anything beyond the dim glow of the running lights. Adrenaline rushed through our veins as we fought to stay in control of the situation. I was afraid that the electronic systems might fail if water flooded the cockpit and found its way below, making it impossible to determine our position. We weren't maintaining a course; we were just trying to survive.

The gale pursued us through the night and into the following day. When we came off watch we stumbled below, grabbed a few crackers to keep something in our stomachs, and crawled into our bunks. The only relief was that with the dawn we were able to see the chaos around us. Even though the helmsman's compass was swinging wildly back and forth, now we knew that our average heading was south. And then we saw the light.

It was dim and distant; we could only see it when the boat was lifted on the crest of a wave. Every time we came up, all eyes strained to find it again through the blinding rain. Soon we realized that the light flashed for two seconds at ten-second intervals. Someone went below to check the charts. Dead ahead of us, forty miles away, was Gibb's Hill Lighthouse at Southampton, Bermuda.

Lighthouses—tall, sturdy, and built to withstand the pounding surf and raging winds—warn passing ships to avoid crashing into rocks or dangerous reefs near shore. Lighthouses have guided sailors through troubled waters for as long as anyone can remember. Seeing that lighthouse was like being held in the arms of a parent or a long-lost friend. Now it didn't matter if our modern equipment failed. All we had to do was not lose sight of it and let nothing keep us from reaching its warm embrace.

At some time, often when we least expect it, we all have to face overwhelming challenges. We are more troubled than we have ever been before; we may doubt that we have what it takes to endure. It is very tempting to give up, yet we have to find the will to keep going. But even when we discover what motivates us, we realize that we can't go the distance alone.

When the unthinkable happens, the lighthouse is hope. Once we find it, we must cling to it with absolute determination, much as our crew did when we saw the light of Gibb's Hill that October afternoon. Hope must be as real, and built on the same solid foundation, as a lighthouse; in that way it is different from optimism or wishful thinking. When we have hope, we discover powers within ourselves we may have never known—the power to make sacrifices, to endure, to heal, and to love. Once we choose hope, everything is possible. We are all on this sea together. But the lighthouse is always there, ready to show us the way home.

*Give humanity hope and it will dare and suffer joyfully,
not counting the cost—hope with laughter on her
banner and on her face the fresh beauty of morning.*
—JOHN ELOF BOODIN

THE FORWARD LOOK

HENRI NOUWEN

We will experience the minutes and hours and days of our lives differently when hope takes up residence. In a letter to Jim Forest, who at the time directed the Fellowship of Reconciliation, Thomas Merton wrote, "The real hope is not in something we think we can do, but in God, who is making something good out of it in some way we cannot see."

Hope is not dependent on peace in the land, justice in the world, and success in the business. Hope is willing to leave unanswered questions unanswered and unknown futures unknown. Hope makes you see God's guiding hand not only in the gentle and pleasant moments but also in the shadows of disappointment and darkness.

No one can truly say with certainty where he or she will be ten or twenty years from now. You do not know if you will be free or in captivity, if you will be honored or despised, if you will have many friends or few, if you will be liked or rejected. But when you hold lightly these dreams and fears, you can be open to receive every day as a new day and to live your life as a unique expression of God's love for humankind.

There is an old expression that says, "As long as there is life, there is hope." As Christians we also say, "As long as there is hope, there is life." Can hope change our lives? Take away our sadness and fatalism? A story helps me answer such questions.

A soldier was captured as a prisoner of war. His captors transported him by train far from his homeland. He felt isolated from country, bereft of family, estranged from anything familiar. His loneliness grew as he continued not to hear anything from home. He could not know that his family was even alive, how his country was faring. He had lost a sense of anything to live for.

But suddenly, unexpectedly, he got a letter. It was smudged, torn at the edges from months of travel. But it said, "We are waiting for you to come home. All is fine here. Don't worry." Everything instantly seemed different. His circumstances had not changed. He did the same difficult labor on the same meager rations, but now he knew someone waited for his release and homecoming. Hope changed his life.

God has written us a letter. The good news of God's revelation in Christ declares to us precisely what we need to hope. Sometimes the words of the Bible do not seem important to us. Or they do not appeal to us. But in those words we hear Christ saying in effect, "I am waiting for you. I am preparing a house for you and there are many rooms in my house." Paul the Apostle tells us, "Be transformed by the renewing of your minds" (Rom. 12:2). We hear a promise and an invitation to a life we could not dream of if all we considered were our own resources.

Therein is the hope that gives us new power to live, new strength. We find a way, even in sadness and illness and even death, never to forget how we can hope.

We catch glimmers of this way to live even while we must admit how dimly we see it and imperfectly we live it. "I am holding onto my conviction that I can trust God," I must tell myself sometimes, "since I cannot say yet say it fully." I dare to say it even when everything is not perfect, when I know others will criticize my actions, when I fear that my limitations will disappoint many—and myself. But still I trust that the truth will shine through, even when I cannot fully grasp it. Still I believe that God will accomplish what I cannot, in God's own grace and unfathomable might.

The paradox of expectation is that those who believe in tomorrow can better live today; those who expect joy to come out of sadness can discover the beginnings of a new life amid the old; those who look forward to the returning Lord can discover him already in their midst. . . . For even while we mourn, we do not forget how our life can ultimately join God's larger dance of life and hope.

Hold fast to dreams, for if dreams die,
life is a broken-winged bird that cannot fly.
—LANGSTON HUGHES

A STRANGE PLACE TO HOPE

CORRIE TEN BOOM

Rank upon rank we stood that hot September morning in 1944, more than a thousand women lining the railroad siding, one unspoken thought among us: *Not Germany!*

Beside me my sister Betsie swayed. I was fifty-two, Betsie fifty-nine. These eight months in a concentration camp since we had been caught concealing Jews in our home had been harder on her. But prisoners though we were, at least till now we had remained in Holland. And now when liberation must come any day, where were they taking us?

Behind us guards were shouting, prodding us with their guns. Instinctively my hand went to the string around my neck. From it, hanging down my back between my shoulder blades, was the small cloth bag that held our Bible, that forbidden book which had not only sustained Betsie and me throughout these months but had given us strength to share with our fellow prisoners. So far we had kept it hidden. But if we should go to Germany . . . we had heard tales of the prison inspections there.

A long line of empty boxcars was rolling slowly past. Now it clanged to a halt and a gaping freight door loomed in front of us. I helped Betsie over the steep side. The dark boxcar grew quickly crowded. We were pressed against the wall. It was a small European freight car, thirty or forty people jammed in it. And still the guards drove women in, pushing, jabbing with their guns. It was only when eighty women were packed inside that the heavy door slid shut and we heard the iron bolts driven into place outside.

Women were sobbing and many fainted, although in the tight-wedged crowd they remained upright. The sun beat down on the motionless train; the temperature in the packed car rose. It was hours before the train gave a sudden lurch and began to move. Almost at once it stopped again, then again crawled forward. The rest of that day and all night long it was the same—stopping, starting, slamming, jerking. Once through a slit in the side of the car, I saw trainmen carrying a length of twisted rail. Maybe the tracks ahead were destroyed. Maybe we would still be in Holland when liberation came.

But at dawn we rolled through the Dutch border town of Emmerich. We were in Germany.

For two more incredible days and two more nights we were carried deeper and deeper into the land of our fears. Worse than the crush of bodies and the filth was the thirst. Two or three times when the train was stopped, the door was slid open a few inches and a pail of water passed in. But we had become animals, incapable of plan. Those near the door got it all.

At last, on the morning of the fourth day, the door was hauled open its full width. Only a handful of very young soldiers was there to order us out and march us off. No more were needed. We could scarcely walk, let alone resist. From the crest of a small hill we saw it, the end of our journey, a vast gray barracks–city surrounded by double concrete walls.

"Ravensbrück!"

Like a whispered curse, the word passed back through the line. This was the notorious women's death camp itself, the very symbol to Dutch hearts of all that was evil. As we stumbled down the hill, I felt the Bible bumping on my back. As long as we had that, I thought, we could face even hell itself. But how could we conceal it through the inspection I knew lay ahead?

It was the middle of the night when Betsie and I reached the processing barracks. And there under the harsh ceiling lights, we saw a dismaying sight. As each woman reached the head of the line, she had to strip off every scrap of clothes, throw them all onto a pile guarded by soldiers, and walk naked past the scrutiny of a dozen guards into the shower room. Coming out of the shower room she wore only the thin regulation prison dress and a pair of shoes.

Our Bible! How could we take it past so many watchful eyes?

"Oh, Betsie!" I began—and then stopped at the sight of her pain-whitened face. As a guard strode by I begged him in German to show us the toilets. He jerked his head in the direction of the shower room. "Use the drain holes!" he snapped.

Timidly Betsie and I stepped out of line and walked forward to the huge room with its row on row of overhead spigots. It was empty, waiting for the next batch of fifty naked and shivering women.

A few minutes later we would return here stripped of everything we possessed. And then we saw them, stacked in a corner: a pile of old wooden benches crawling with cockroaches, but to us the furniture of heaven itself.

In an instant I had slipped the little bag over my head and stuffed it behind the benches.

And so it was that when we were herded into that room ten minutes later, we were not poor, but rich. Rich in the care of him who was God even of Ravensbrück.

Of course when I put on the flimsy prison dress, the Bible bulged beneath it. But that was his business, not mine. At the exit, guards were feeling every prisoner, front, back and sides. The woman ahead of me was searched. Behind me, Betsie was searched. They did not touch or even look at me.

Outside the building was a second ordeal, another line of guards examining each prisoner again. I slowed down as I reached them, but the captain shoved me roughly by the shoulder. "Move along! You're holding up the line!"

So Betsie and I came to our barracks at Ravensbrück. Before long we were holding clandestine Bible study groups for an ever-growing group of believers, and Barracks 28 became known throughout the camp as "the crazy place, where they hope."

Yes, hoped, in spite of all that human madness could do. We had learned that a stronger power had the final word, even here.

Everybody lives for something better to come.
—Author Unknown

A Corsage of Purple Flowers

Charles Hart

My granddad had a story for everything. One of his favorites was about a farmer who would take any bet. Finally, he made a crazy wager: he bet he could lift a full-grown steer. He just wanted eighteen months to prove it.

The farmer knew he could lift a newborn calf. He'd done it before, and he expected he could lift it the second day too. The calf might gain a few pounds a day, but the farmer reasoned his strength might grow at the same rate, as long as he kept picking up the calf. Granddad said the farmer went out to the corral every morning, just to lift that calf. The calf kept getting heavier and the farmer—well, he just strained a little harder every day.

Granddad never finished this tale or told anyone how it was supposed to end. He just grinned and let the listeners draw their own conclusions. He figured the imagination was more powerful than any punch line. He just left us thinking about that farmer.

As a child, I wanted to know this story's outcome. I bet against the farmer. Common sense says this experiment wouldn't work. He'd break his back trying!

On the other hand, why not? There are so many examples of adjustment and accommodation in the world, it's hard to see boundaries to reality or to keep up with technology's frontiers. Why shouldn't we believe in the impossible? How much can a person accomplish with faith and perseverance?

Imagine the farmer eighteen months later. His buddies have joined him at the corral, waiting to see him fail or break his back. They grow quiet as he parades into the corral, a full-grown steer on his lead. As the others gape in astonishment, he proudly hoists the animal and collects his bets.

Today, I like this second ending. It raises possibilities above predictions, a belief that dreams can come true and that people are stronger than they think. This interpretation means more to me than the harsher one. It helps me understand my own life and the challenge of living with two generations of autism.

My attitude toward autism began in the 1940s. By the age of four, I knew my brother Scott was our secret. His pain and the pain of him were too private to share with others. My sisters and I left as soon as we could, marrying young or attending college across the country. Years later, I would hear a psychologist classify our behavior as "siblings' flight." It was flight all right, but Scott hadn't chased us away. Fear, shame, and confusion had made our home unbearable.

Early on, I thought Scott's disability was the worst curse a family could suffer. I'd seen my parents break under the burden and knew I couldn't follow. Could it happen again? Was it possible that I might father a child who never grows up? This fear plagued me in my twenties, but after five years of marriage, my wife and I conceived our first child.

At Ted's birth, I nagged the doctor for reassurance. Ted passed every screening and he earned a nine out of ten on the newborn scale. We enjoyed the infancy so much, we weren't in a hurry to see it pass.

By Ted's second birthday, we noticed little quirks, eccentricities that suggested he was different. His language was odd. He didn't play with other children. His scores on developmental charts started to slip. By his third birthday, we confronted the truth: our son was different and it wasn't a difference we had chosen.

Like many parents, we suffered through a series of diagnoses that seemed more like professional guesses: brain damaged, neurologically impaired, and finally, autistic—the adjective used to describe Scott's problem. We searched for help, ways to "fix" Ted; but the more we learned, the less we hoped. It looked like my worst nightmare had come true: my second family seemed as doomed as my first.

On the positive side, my wife and I had resources my parents had never known. We had steady employment, better education, and access to a university-based training center. Furthermore, society had begun to recognize the rights and needs of people with disabilities. Unlike Scott, who had been born in the 1920s, my child wouldn't have to stay hidden in the home. The law guaranteed him an education. Medical understanding had progressed too.

It took awhile to overcome all the fears from my childhood. But we discovered we weren't alone, our son wasn't hopeless—and neither was my brother. Concern for my son's welfare made me more sensitive to my brother's feelings. I began to see Scott in another light, and the vision startled me. It seemed clearer and more honest than my earlier view. All those years, we had overlooked Scott's needs. We were too eager to blame someone else for our problems.

Revisiting the past, I realized we had it all wrong: *Scott hadn't been our problem; we were his!* Confronting those feelings hurt, but the pain brought a rush of adrenaline and determination. It hit me like a bolt of lightning: *Whether something is a curse or a blessing depends on interpretation.*

I could choose to interpret my son's disability as I wanted. Would I see it as a burden, a challenge, or an opportunity? It was up to me: I had to play the hand I'd been dealt, but how I played it was up to me!

During what sometimes seemed a long and tortuous childhood, my wife and I struggled to understand Ted and tried not to neglect his younger brother in the process. Raising two sons with such different needs put us to the test. We stumbled through their childhoods, waiting for graduation like a light promised at the end of the tunnel.

Ted's twenty-second birthday found us pretty well prepared. For years we'd worked toward this transition, his passage into the adult world. He'd graduate at the end of the year. Between his part-time jobs and federal assistance, he'd have a reasonable income. His supervisors knew him well and had trained him during student internships. We even fixed up a basement apartment for him.

We thought everything was planned for graduation, but Ted didn't. That spring, in his senior year, he caught us off guard with his announcement: "I'm going to the prom."

He was going to the prom! He'd thought about it for years. All he needed was a date. But he simply couldn't get a date on his own. Some of the cheerleaders called him "cute" and tolerated his attention at assemblies, but none would actually date him.

A family friend had a daughter less than a year older than our son. She and Ted had already met through their families, and, in spite of educational differences, they liked and trusted one another. Jennifer understood what prom night meant to Ted, so she agreed to take a formal out of storage and fly across the country.

As prom night approached, we helped Ted prepare. We wanted his experience to be as special as we had believed ours was a generation ago. We dusted off the etiquette book and the family tuxedo. Ted agreed to let me chauffeur him and Jennifer in the family car. He even planned their dinner before the dance. Only one detail remained: the floral tribute, the corsage.

In prom culture, Jennifer had to wear flowers, and they had to come from Ted. It was a very tender symbol, because this young man might never have occasion to present a woman with flowers again. If I'd picked up the phone, I could have ordered that corsage in two minutes flat. But that would have taken the opportunity away from Ted. He needed that experience and I wanted him to have it. So we prepared Ted to buy his date's flowers.

First we rehearsed Ted's interview with Jennifer, so that he could ask what color she planned to wear and whether she wanted flowers on her wrist or on her shoulder. Via long-distance, she told him she wanted a wrist corsage to accent a black dress. Next we researched flowers using the encyclopedia. We looked at gardenias, roses, and orchids, noting their colors. Finally, Ted felt confident enough to make a choice.

Preparing for the trip to the florist, Ted wanted to role play. He likes to have a planned script. Practicing the words at home makes them easier to say in another setting. Ted gave me the florist's role, so I invited him into my imaginary shop;

"Good afternoon. What can I do for you?"

"I want to buy a corsage," he answered.

"Not really." I interrupted to explain that, if he "bought" a corsage on Wednesday, it would look pretty stale and wilted on Saturday night. "You don't want to buy a corsage today, you want to order one," I prompted.

We rehearsed until Ted seemed letter perfect. When he had the script down, we strolled to our neighborhood florist. As soon as the little bell on the door stopped jangling, Ted looked like he was trapped. The air was heavy with the smell of flowers and spice.

Near the back, a single clerk sorted through receipts and orders. Hearing the door, she stopped filing and turned her attention to us. I waited for Ted to speak, looking at him expectantly. It grew very quiet in the shop, then he cleared his throat. His entire body had grown rigid. He drew his face into a grimace and blurted out, "I'm Ted. I'm here to rent the purple flowers."

The clerk looked startled. She glanced at me as I calmly prompted, "Let's try that again, Ted."

He drew a couple of deep breaths and furrowed his brows. "Look at her and tell her what you want to order," I suggested.

He stumbled a few more times before getting back on track. Finally, by staying calm and speaking slowly, Ted was able to answer all of the clerk's questions:

He wanted a corsage for Saturday. His date wanted to wear it on her wrist. He preferred purple or lavender roses. He'd pay when he picked it up Saturday afternoon.

After twenty-two years, I had grown accustomed to Ted's responses. I hadn't expected the clerk's reaction.

"You have a lot of patience," she said. "I could never be so patient. "

At first bewildered, she had changed to sympathy, then to admiration. But she was admiring the wrong person! Unknown to the clerk, this young man had climbed mountains of barriers and swam oceans of confusion, just to reach this point. Saturday night wouldn't find him working a jigsaw puzzle as his uncle had spent his youth. Ted was going to the prom!

Back home, I told my wife about the experience. I'd never thought of myself as patient. Quite the contrary. It shocked me to hear a stranger say, "You have a lot of patience."

No! I'd wanted to shout. *This isn't patience; this is understanding.* My son, not I, deserved credit for patience. He has to labor the pathways we take for granted; he has to struggle upstream toward a life the rest of us take for granted. It amazed me that someone would call me patient instead of admiring my son's greater fortitude

My wife pointed out that the clerk's response had been more normal than either Ted's or mine. She suggested that, over time and without realizing it, I'd developed listening skills that looked like patience to others. She reminded me that others don't see our relationship in context. They don't see the history and the struggle, only the first impression, the here and now.

On prom night I dropped Ted and Jennifer at the dance and gave them taxi fare for the ride back. At home we phoned my father-in-law, letting him know that his most handsome grandson had gone to the prom. Then I called a sister in Albuquerque. We talked about our brother's stunted life and the amazing progress Ted had already made. We cried.

I keep a photo from the dance on my desk. Jennifer stands beside Ted. On her wrist she wears a corsage of lavender roses. That image freezes time.

Before I knew he faced special challenges, I had fairly typical ambitions for my son. I hoped my children would be better, more successful versions of my wife and myself. That wasn't a very exciting goal, but comfortable, normal. I couldn't predict that he'd wrench me from the mainstream and lead me in a more interesting direction, his personal path. To keep up with Ted I had to slow down. He taught me that some people need more time. They don't all accelerate under stress or perform under pressure.

When my son was very young, he was easy to lift. It seemed appropriate to make decisions for him, choosing clothes, scheduling activities, setting behavior rules. It's harder now. So, whenever I try to influence him, shape consumer patterns or social behavior, I'd better be certain it's for his best interest, not my peace of mind.

Twenty years ago I didn't think I could cope with a son's disability. It had never occurred to me that I could become a stronger person, that I would discover meaning and direction for my own life through the challenge of another person. I hadn't done anything extraordinary, just lifted my calf each day. Granddad was right not to finish the story. He knew the ending depends on the listener. We write our own endings.

Thou, which hast shewed me great and sore troubles,
shalt quicken me again, and shalt bring me up again
from the depths of the earth.

—PSALM 71:20

VOICES IN THE DARKNESS

JAN KILIC

A stand at the window and look out into the yard at our daughter Natalie playing on the jungle gym. When she sees me, her eyes light up, and she waves. My right arm is still partially paralyzed, so I lift it with my left hand to wave back. "Hi, Mommy!" she calls.

Easter is coming, and I cannot help but think of those in our family who are no longer here to share it with us: Natalie's four brothers and sisters and her paternal grandparents. All of them dead as a result of a huge earthquake last August in Turkey.

Not a day goes by that I don't miss talking to my father- and mother-in-law, miss holding my children and hugging them close to me. Yet when I look back on everything that has happened, I see how it is that I have been able to go on, even after losing so many people I love.

Last summer my husband, Bobby, and I decided to take our children to Turkey to meet his relatives. Bobby's parents had immigrated to America years ago, but they still had family in Istanbul. They had bought a vacation getaway, a condominium right on the beach in Yalova, a resort town south of the city, and they'd invited us to spend a few weeks with them. I went over first, in mid-August, with the children. They were looking forward to their daddy joining us in a week.

On the night of August 16, I tucked the kids in as usual. First the girls, in the bedroom next to mine: five-year-old Jennifer, three-year-old Natalie, and baby Katie. Then the boys, Jeffrey, six, and David, two, on a cot in my room. A little later I said good-night to Bobby's folks and climbed into bed myself. I fell into a sound sleep.

A roar woke me, a terrible sound I will never forget. Next came a jarring thud as the bed gave way. Then a shower of debris. What was happening?

The children! In the dark I groped for the cot beside my bed. "Jeffrey! David!" I felt splintered wood, then the metal frame of the cot. There! My hand touched Jeffrey's pajama sleeve. But he didn't move.

I struggled to my feet. "Jennifer! Natalie! Katie!"

Before I heard an answer, the floor trembled and dropped from beneath me. Another grinding roar. Something tremendously heavy hit my back, pinning me across the fallen cot, my chest pressed against its frame, my face inches from the floor. Neither of the boys made a sound.

Plaster rained down on me. I heard a muffled cry. "Jan!" My father-in-law's voice! "Nizam!" I yelled back to him.

"Can you hear me, Jan?" he asked. "It's an earthquake!"

Choking on plaster dust, I shouted, "Can you reach the girls?" No. "Turkan?" Again, no. My mother-in-law, he believed, was alive but badly injured.

The weight on my back was squeezing the breath out of me, and I felt the edges of my vision closing in. *Stay awake!* I told myself. *Think of something good.* I pictured myself at home in Georgia with Bobby and the children. Safe in our house with the jungle gym outside where the kids loved to play.

The floor shifted once more. Rubble pelted my back. Had the entire building collapsed? Nizam said something to his wife in Turkish. Then he told me in English: He didn't know about Jennifer and the baby, but he thought he'd heard Natalie crying.

"Nat—" I managed to gasp before a fit of coughing shook me.

My father-in-law spoke again. "Someone will come, Jan." His voice was so strong and calm. "Help will come."

My mother-in-law cried out and I caught the word *Allah*. I began praying too, there in the dark. *Jesus, dear Jesus, please be with us.*

I couldn't feel anything with my right hand, but I wiggled the fingers of my left hand to keep the blood moving. I stopped when they closed over Jeffrey's pajamas. He lay still, frighteningly still. I shut my eyes, trying to block out the terrible images of what might have happened to my children.

"Mommy!" The cry jolted me out of the dark, semiconscious fog I'd drifted into. Had I been dreaming of home? No, that was my Natalie calling me!

"Mommy," she moaned, "I'm thirsty."

"Natalie!" I tried to shout. "Sweetie, I'm right here!" But chalky dust filled my mouth and only a rasp came out.

My children, Lord, please . . . I slipped into a deep prayer that went beyond words. *Dear Jesus* . . . I lost consciousness repeating his name.

When I woke next, I felt Jeffrey's body cold beneath my hand. How long had we been trapped here? There were sounds outside, people shouting. I heard Nizam's voice, weaker now, too soft for me to catch what he was saying. *Stay with us, Jesus,* I prayed. *Don't let me give up.*

I forced my mind away from the present, back to the past, to my student days at the University of Alabama, where Bobby and I had met and fallen in love. He was a medical student; I, an undergraduate in electrical engineering. I remembered how I'd liked Bobby's parents right away. They were both pediatricians, and their three sons all became doctors too. I wondered who our kids would take after.

Our children. Jeffrey, a wonderful big brother, always looking out for the little ones. Lively, outgoing Jennifer, who made friends with everyone. Natalie, with her tenderness toward the baby. David, racing his Big Wheel tricycle down the driveway. And Katie, such a happy, good-natured baby . . .

"Jan," Nizam gasped. "Hold on, Jan! They're coming to get us."

Shouts. A scraping noise. Nizam calling to someone in Turkish. More men shouting, then what sounded like shovels digging. I must have fainted. Suddenly there was light, just inches from my face. I heard an English word. "Gas." A gas leak! I could smell the fumes. The digging would have to stop till the gas could be shut off. I could hear the rescuers moving away, their voices fading.

One, though, was still near. A young man, speaking Turkish. I drifted in and out of consciousness. Every now and again, the young man's voice came, close by, pulling me back, giving me hope.

Hammering. A ratcheting sound. I felt the crushing weight on my back ease. Then strong hands were lifting me, carrying me over piles of rubble, and placing me gently into the rear of a car. As we drove off, I saw the massive ruin that had once been the vacation home for my in-laws, for hundreds of people. "The children," I murmured. "Did you find them? Nizam? Turkan?"

"Don't talk," someone said. "Rest."

It wasn't until much later, in the hospital with broken vertebrae and a paralyzed right arm, that I learned what had become of our family. Jeffrey, Jennifer, David, and Katie had died instantly. By the time rescuers had reached Nizam, he was gone as well. Turkan was alive, but barely hanging on. No one had been able to find Natalie.

Thirty-six hours after the earthquake, cleanup crews began bulldozing the wreck of the condo. A workman saw a tiny puff of dust float up and stopped to investigate. It turned out to be Natalie's breath stirring the air. She came away with only a black eye. A miracle. Truly a miracle. A small yet unmistakable ray of hope cutting through the darkness.

Now, months after the earthquake, I'm in our house in Marietta, waiting for Bobby to come home from work so we can have dinner together as a family. A little earlier Natalie had skipped in. "Can I go out and play, Mommy? Just till Daddy gets home?" I said yes, though I would rather have had her sit and talk with me.

It reminds me of what kept me alive for the long hours I was buried in the rubble in Yalova. Every time I'd felt myself slipping away, someone's voice would bring me back. Nizam, who kept encouraging me to hold on. Turkan, who, in praying, spurred me to do the same. Natalie, who called to me and drew me back to consciousness. The young Turkish man who risked his life to stay and comfort me until other rescuers could dig me out.

Through those voices, in them and beyond them, there was another voice. The voice of Jesus, bringing Easter's message of life into that scene of devastation and death. And it is his voice that now leads me through the darkness when my grief seems more than I can bear.

Life, I think as I watch Natalie climb higher on the jungle gym, is always Jesus' message. He bears our deepest pain for us so we can go on living—abundantly— here on earth. And he promises us, beyond the grave, a new life that never ends.

I hear Bobby's car in the driveway. A minute later he's scooping Natalie up and carrying her inside the house.

As I go to meet them, through the open window a breeze drifts in, gentle as a baby's breath against my skin. I think about the babies I will soon be holding—the Turkish boy and girl, born shortly after the earthquake, whom Bobby and I are applying to adopt. We hope to see our children playing on the jungle gym in our yard again one day, laughing with their sister Natalie. Yes, we hope.

Hope is faith holding out its hand in the dark.
—George Iles

THE BEST WORD OF ALL

ROBERTA MESSNER

"*loriferous.* F-L-O-R-I-F-E-R-O-U-S. *Floriferous.*"

"Correct," Mama said, consulting my dog-eared copy of *Words of the Champions* open in her lap. "Now try *staphylococcus.*"

I was twelve years old, and after four years of being the runner-up in our grade school competition, I had qualified for the spelling-bee regional competition. At last my dream was on the verge of coming true. All I had to do was win the regionals, and Mama and I would get an all-expenses-paid trip to Washington, D.C., on the Chesapeake & Ohio Railroad.

We practiced out on the front porch steps. Mama shelled half-runner beans and drilled me on words like *insouciant* and *ephemera.* "Sound out the syllables and picture how the letters look in your mind," Mama said. "That's the secret." But all I could really picture was that railroad trip. I could see us climbing aboard the big train, settling back in the plush seats and whizzing through the countryside to glory in Washington, D.C. We would have a dinner fit for queens in the dining car, served on cream-colored china embossed with the C&O's adorable Chessie-cat logo.

My dreams were imaginative, elevating, grandiose—all words I could spell perfectly. *Dear God,* I prayed, *I want that train ride so much. It'll be my first big trip.* Then my mind would leap eagerly into the future. *And when I grow up I'll go to college and maybe I'll be a scientist or a foreign correspondent . . . or maybe even a famous actress.*

Finally the big day arrived. That Saturday morning in the auditorium I made my way to my assigned place onstage and straightened the cardboard placard around my neck that read "West Junior High." I waved to Mama and Daddy in the audience as the first round began. One by one the other contestants went to the microphone to spell the words called out by the announcer.

Giraffe. Mentor. Cousin. Why, these words were a breeze! At last it was my turn. With a confident swish of the green skirt I'd made in sewing class, I stepped up to the microphone. Mama leaned forward in her seat.

"*Biscuit,*" the announcer said, looking up at me. Easy! There was no need to ask him to define that word or use it in a sentence. I formed a picture in my mind. I could see the bright blue-and-yellow box of mix on our kitchen counter just as clear as day. Quick as a wink I spelled out "B-I-S-Q-U-I-C-K."

There was a gasp from the audience. Someone actually said, "Oh, no." The awful buzzer sounded. My stomach turned. I was O-U-T, *out.*

I felt everyone's eyes bore into me. My cheeks burned. I stumbled to the back of the auditorium, where Mama appeared and gently steered me out to the parking lot. "Don't you worry, honey," she said. "Anybody could make a mistake like that." On the way home we had to stop at the railroad crossing as a long, sleek train zoomed by us. "Never mind, Roberta," Mama said to me. "We'll ride that train yet."

I graduated to eighth grade, too old to enter the spelling bee again. Even if I could have, though, something bigger happened to me that year, something that changed my life. One morning before school, I leaned over to lace up my shoe and suddenly blacked out. When I came to, I was lying on the rug, Mama's worried face above me. She took me right to the doctor. He couldn't figure out what was wrong and sent me home to bed. Over the next few weeks my right eye began to bulge. After several more visits to different doctors in town, Mama explained that I had a tumor near my eye and we needed to go to a big medical center in Cleveland to learn more about it. I had never been so far from home and the idea of a hospital was scary. "I'll be with you the whole time," Mama said. "And honey, guess what? You and I will go there on the train."

Mama showed me on the map the towns the train would pass through, and I cut a picture of the railroad's Chessie-cat logo out of a magazine advertisement and taped it to my mirror so when I looked, I saw the Chessie cat instead of my bulging eye.

The next week Daddy drove us to the Chesapeake & Ohio Railroad station. I wore white gloves and clutched my little pink suitcase tightly. The train approached, getting bigger and bigger. I reached for Mama's hand as the huge locomotive stopped with a hiss.

Daddy helped us aboard, hoisted our suitcases onto the rack above, and Mama and I spread out over the plush blue seats. I waved with all my might as we pulled out of the station. The train picked up speed, and I pressed my face to the glass and watched the countryside roll by.

Mama and I went to the dining car and sat at a table covered with a white cloth. In the center of each cream-colored plate was the famous C&O Railroad Chessie cat, with the words "Sleep like a kitten" beneath. And after the delicious meal we snoozed soundly indeed.

That turned out to be the first of a half-dozen rides Mama and I took to Cleveland so I could be tested and treated for my mystery illness. The doctors puzzled over how to treat my tumor. Mama slept in a chair right beside my bed, and I had various roommates. I took schoolwork with me so I was able to keep up with my classes.

Even though I didn't care much for being sick and looking strange, I found myself enjoying visiting other patients. I walked the corridors, bringing water and tissues to much sicker people who couldn't get out of their beds and sharing my crayons with other kids. I helped a lady with her walker, cleaned some meal trays, and once pushed the book cart. It felt good to do something besides wait for test results.

One day as I sat in bed working on my arithmetic homework, a new doctor appeared in the doorway and beckoned to Mama.

I pretended to be engrossed in my homework while he lowered his voice and talked to Mama. "Your daughter has a condition called neurofibromatosis," he said.

He talked to Mama some more, and although I couldn't make out all of what he said, this part I heard: "Your little girl probably shouldn't make any big plans for her life, like going to college or having a career," he said. "Dealing with this disease is going to take up a good deal of her time and energy."

I felt the same kind of sinking feeling I had after missing the word at the spelling bee. But it was worse. A lot worse. What about all my dreams of having an exciting, wonderful life? Would I have to give those up too? I bit my lip to keep from crying.

One look at my face and Mama knew I'd overheard. She came right over and put her arm around me. "Honey, doctors don't know everything," she said. "Even if your life doesn't work out exactly the way you hoped, God still has plans for you. Whenever life takes away a possibility, God replaces it with something better. Remember how you thought you'd never have a train ride when you missed that word in the spelling bee?" she said. "Well, just look at all the wonderful trips we've taken since then. Disappointments aren't an end. They just clear the way for the Lord to guide us to something even more wonderful."

We packed up and got ready to go home. The morning of our departure I helped my nine-year-old roommate, Karen, who was partially paralyzed from a brain tumor, with her breakfast tray. I spread a napkin in her lap, peeled back the lid on her juice, and inserted straw in her milk carton. "You're getting stronger every day," I reassured her, spreading her strawberry jam. "Thanks for taking care of me," she said.

That's when it struck me: I was good at taking care of people, from the kids I colored pictures with to the adults to whom I brought glasses of water. And no matter how many tumors I got, I could still do that. I could become a nurse! All my old glamorous aspirations faded into the background. Nothing could beat how good it felt to help people. And I'd be an even better nurse because I knew what it felt like to need one.

Dreams didn't die, they changed into something better, just like Mama had promised me.

Mama walked in with my discharge papers. "What's that you're fixing for Karen?" she asked.

"It's a biscuit," I said, "spelled B-I-S-Q-U-I-C-K." Mama and I laughed. I said goodbye to Karen, and we boarded the train back home.

Despite my illness, I did go on to college and become a nurse. I've had my share of other disappointments, but time and again God has led me to something better. In the end, one of the simplest words Mama taught me has meant the most of all—H-O-P-E.

. . . The needy shall not always be forgotten. . . .
—PSALM 9:18

THE AFTERGLOW

MARJORIE HOLMES

My mother always savored sunsets until the last lingering glow had faded from our Iowa sky.

"Just look at that sunset now!" Mother was always urging us. "Isn't that the most beautiful sky you've ever seen?"

Then, after supper when the bright hues had melted into the dusk and there was nothing left of the sunset but a last stubborn band of burning rose, she would return to the porch a minute and stand there, arms wrapped in her apron against the chill, and murmur: "The afterglow means hope."

What could hope possibly mean to this middle-aged married woman whose dreams must surely all be behind her?

I was puzzled. I sensed her hopes but dimly: that the problems of her family would be resolved, wounds healed, frictions cease, worries vanish . . . the doctor's report would be favorable . . . my brother wouldn't have to have an operation, after all . . . that new company would be hiring soon, and Dad would land a better job . . . there would at last be enough money to go around . . . her children's turbulent lives would get straightened out—the boys would find themselves.

Hope? What did it mean to her? It spoke of that marvelous ingredient that keeps men going—something that is almost as vital to man as love—his God-given hope, his belief in tomorrow, his bright expectations that refuse to die.

It was surely what the Lord Himself was talking about when He counseled His followers to be of good cheer, not to despair.

My mother gave her children the gift of sunsets. But an even greater gift was her gift of the afterglow: the message she read in those remaining embers, burning like little fires of faith long after the sunset itself was gone, a lighted bridge across the coming darkness to the stars, "The afterglow means hope."

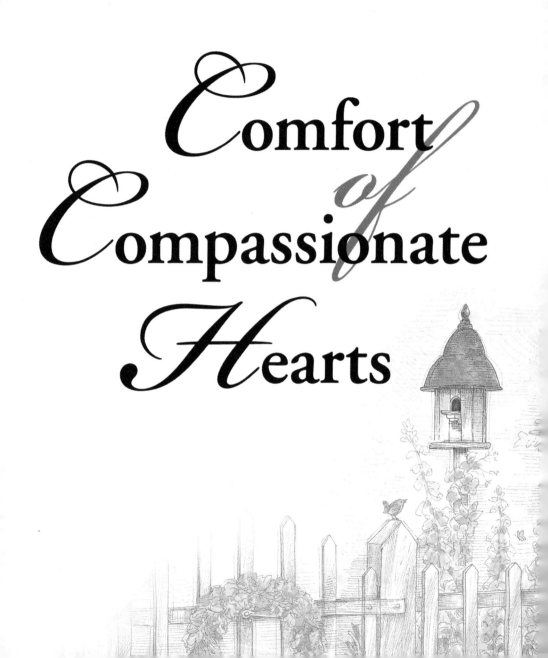

Comfort of Compassionate Hearts

*Little things seem nothing, but they give peace,
like those meadow flowers which individually seem
odorless but all together perfume the air.*
—GEORGE BERNANOS

FLOWERS OF COMPASSION

KATHLEEN TREANOR WITH CANDY CHAND

P eople from around the world reached out with loving arms, offering whatever they could—a shoulder to cry on, a kind word, a prayer. Even the U.S. Postal Service went substantially above and beyond their call of duty. One envelope arrived safely from Ireland with only the following address: "To the Parents of Ashley Eckles who was killed in the bombing." I opened each letter and read every word.

There were other letters from individuals bearing our last name. We may never know if we're related, but the similarity caused them to connect with our plight and to reach out with compassion.

The letters from children were the most heart-wrenching. They brought up the same question I'd asked myself so many times before—Why?

Each one tried to offer comfort, each allowed me to let go of a little more pain. I didn't understand why these people were writing to me, but I was thankful for their words.

The most helpful letters I received were from mothers, and grandmothers, who'd also lost a child. They tried to prepare me for the road ahead.

The letters kept coming. Each one helped me to realize how much people cared.

Many gifts came through the mail. One was from Sheila, who lost her husband tragically and was having trouble coping. She sent her "Wings of Hope," a beautiful gold charm of angel wings that she designed and marketed herself.

I was amazed by the number of letters that poured in. Each time I opened one, I realized how much people wanted to offer hope.

I've stored each letter carefully away for safekeeping. Along with the correspondence came many trinkets, statuettes, handmade items, jewelry, and books. I treasured the books the most. I read each one carefully, line by line, hoping for a glimmer of understanding. There were days when the kindness from strangers became my sanity, the very thing that kept me going. But I was seldom able to extend beyond my own grief to thank them for their compassion.

The letters from those who'd experienced loss were the most helpful. They assured me, line by line, it was okay to feel the way I did. Each time someone reached out, my burden became a little bit lighter. I began to understand the expression, "Misery loves company." Their words offered comfort, empathy, and understanding, born simply from the fact they'd travelled that road before me.

From around the world compassionate people sowed fragile seeds of faith. In turn, I've reaped a bountiful harvest of blessings. Thanks to my earth angels, what was meant for evil miraculously become much more—a beautiful, God-inspired tapestry of love.

God has created mankind for fellowship,
and not for solitariness.
—MARTIN LUTHER

LIFE STEPS

GLORIA HAYNES

reporter for the only newspaper in Breckinridge County, Kentucky, I stood alongside the track to photograph participants in the Relay for Life. Sponsored by the American Cancer Society, the annual event is designed to raise money for research. The turnout was huge. But cancer was something I didn't want to think about. My mother had died of lung cancer, and I'd spent the ten years since avoiding anything having to do with the dreaded disease. Now here I was surrounded by it. And these people—strangers to each other—actually wanted to be here. What could they possibly do for each other? Why would these people want to participate in something as sad as this?

"Please take your seats around the track, ladies and gentlemen," a man's voice boomed over the loudspeakers. "We will now begin our survivors' lap."

I went over to the bleachers, determined to finish my roll of film and go home. People strolled steadily past me. All of these people are survivors? A familiar bitterness welled up inside me. Dad had died two years before Mom, suddenly, of a heart attack. The shock of it was hard to get past. But Mom's death, a long and agonizing ordeal, seemed ever the more unfair. I kept her company, read to her, tried to make her comfortable. But in the end, really, there was not a thing I could do for her. I had felt helpless and frustrated.

The announcer's voice boomed as the survivors left the track: "In the caregivers' lap, you are invited to walk in honor of the loved one you cared for and the love you put into caring for that person."

Music poured from the speakers. I remembered how frightened and alone I'd felt that last year of Mom's illness. I kept my feelings to myself and did what I had to do to. Every day I asked God for strength, and he gave it to me.

I looked out at the caregivers walking, remembering their loved ones. *God, I need you now too. I'm still struggling to stay strong these ten years later.* But I couldn't hold my grief inside anymore. I sat down on the bleachers and cried.

I felt warm arms encircle me, and I looked up. It was a woman, a stranger. She pulled me toward her. I laid my head on her shoulder and cried some more, as if I had known her all my life. Ten years of pent-up emotion poured out of me. Finally, I pulled away and looked into the woman's kind face.

"I'm crying because of my mother," I said. "Who are you here for?"

She wiped a tear from my cheek. "You, I guess." She hugged me hard, then mixed back into the crowd of caregivers on the track.

I can't tell you exactly what this woman looked like or even the color of her hair. But I believe she was right. She was there for me that day. Because God has many ways of giving us strength. Sometimes it's in the form of other people. And that's what everybody was doing at the Relay for Life. They were all angels, strengthening one another.

An ounce of help is better than a pound of preaching.
—EDWARD BULWER-LYTTON

WISE AND WINSOME

GIGI GRAHAM TCHIVIDJIAN

At was a warm, balmy north Florida evening. The waves gently lapped the white sand beach outside of our hotel room and the palm fronds rustled against the window as we dressed for dinner.

Mother was to be interviewed at an event honoring a prestigious medical institution. During the interview she answered questions about her childhood in China, her high school years in North Korea, and then her marriage to, and her life with, my daddy, Billy Graham. She went on to discuss her years as a mother; her joys as well as her difficulties. She talked about the times of having to make decisions when Daddy was away preaching, sometimes tough decisions, alone. She also shared about the trying, difficult years when she had to deal with her prodigals.

After dinner, many came up to speak and to thank her for her honest, open sharing.

I noticed one distinguished, well-dressed woman who hung back, waiting for a chance to speak. Tension was evident and she struggled to hold back the tears. When the crowd cleared, she approached Mother timidly, hesitantly.

"My son died of an overdose of drugs," she said with difficulty. "Do you think I will see him again in heaven?"

Of course, Mother didn't know any of the details, but she saw before her a mother with a very heavy heart. So she answered, "If you heard a timid knock on your door one day, and you answered the knock only to find your child standing there, bruised, wounded, bleeding, dirty, and tattered, what would you do? Slam the door in his face? Or would you throw open the door and welcome him into your arms?"

Suddenly, this mother's face registered relief. I saw the load lift from her shoulders as the tears flowed down her cheeks because she knew she was hearing from a mother who knew what it was like to have a prodigal. They hugged each other, and the woman turned and disappeared into the crowd.

A friend loveth at all times,
and a brother is born for adversity.
—PROVERBS 17:17

BESIDE THE WHISPERING WATERS

MARTHA A. HARDIN

Another beautiful day, one in a long line of what should have been perfect fall days. But I could barely appreciate it. That was not like me. Autumn had always been my favorite time of year—the crispness in the air, the colors of the leaves, kids knocking at the door on Halloween, family gathered together at Thanksgiving. In the fall of 1988, though, there was no joy in my life, no laughter. The sense of invigoration I usually felt was missing, and the changing of the seasons seemed only to add to my despair.

Just four months earlier my son David had died of an aneurysm. He was twenty-four years old. I couldn't understand why he'd died, and it was nearly more than I could stand. My mind spun like a movie at the end of its reel. Nothing at all made much sense to me anymore. Especially my prayers. I'd prayed since David was a baby, asking that he and his brother would grow up to be happy, healthy, and successful men. But now one of my sons was gone. Had God even paid attention to those prayers?

I kept searching for David. I'd look for him in crowds. I'd listen for his car in the driveway. I'd strain to hear his voice.

My husband and son tried to help me cope, but they had their own grief to struggle with. And mine was that of a mother for her child. None of my friends had lost a child. They couldn't conceive of what I was going through. I knew they cared about me, but not one could bring herself even to mention David's name around me, let alone talk about him. Yet that's what I longed to do. I felt so alone, even more so when I was in a room full of people who didn't understand the depth of my despair.

I just about stopped socializing. During my time by myself I often wished I could join David. But I'd feel guilty at the thought, knowing I still had family here too. So I plodded along from day to day, somehow managing to will myself out of bed each morning. The hours dragged by, and sometimes the only thing that kept me going was thinking about David: how handsome and smart he was, how beautifully he sang and played the piano and saxophone, how kind he could be.

Every single afternoon I headed to Restland Memorial Park, so I could spend some time at his graveside. On weekends I stopped at a flower shop for a bouquet. It gave me a feeling of doing something for David.

One Saturday, though, I skipped visiting the cemetery so I could do some grocery shopping. I was reaching for a can on a shelf when the strangest feeling came over me. It hit me so hard that I thought it was a panic attack. But after that initial jolt, I realized it wasn't panic I was feeling. No, it was an irresistible urge. A voice in my head kept saying, *Go to the cemetery.* I was getting to the end of my shopping list; my cart was nearly full. But I couldn't help myself. I left the groceries there in the middle of the aisle, ran from the store, and got into my car. I headed straight for Restland, the car seeming to drive itself.

I parked at the edge of Whispering Waters, the section we'd chosen for David. There was a lovely little stream and a waterfall that we thought he would have liked. I got out of the car and looked around. *Why this urge?* I wondered. Nothing seemed out of the ordinary; David's grave and headstone, the flowers—all were just as I'd left them the day before.

Why do you keep coming here? I chastised. *What do you expect to find?* Certainly not David. Leaves had fallen on his grave. Even my favorite season couldn't give me comfort. Instead it just pointed out all the sadness and death around me. Dropping to my knees by the headstone, I sobbed. From somewhere deep inside the words came, inexplicably, and as strange and powerful as the urge that had overtaken me in the supermarket: "God, where are you? I'm all alone here, and I can't find what I'm looking for."

Just moments later, I felt hands on my shoulders. I turned and looked up. A woman stood above me with tears on her cheeks. She said, "I know how you feel. My daughter died of breast cancer not even a year ago. She was just thirty-seven, and she left a two-and-a-half-year-old son. I hurt just like you. It gets easier, but it never goes away."

After all the months alone, all the time spent thinking no one could understand my overwhelming sorrow, finally here was someone who knew it intimately. I got up to look at her. I could hardly believe the woman was real. But she was. We held each other, sadness and relief washing over me.

Her name was Louise, she told me as we sat on the stone bench by David's grave. She talked all about her daughter, who'd had so much to live for and had wanted nothing more than to see her own son grow up. Just what I'd wanted. I told Louise about my prayers. Together we cried, for our children and for ourselves. We sat on that stone bench together for two hours.

That day was the beginning of my friendship with Louise. I was comfortable with her. She was one of those people who could talk openly about her grief. It must have lessened her burden some.

We would talk and talk for hours, about all sorts of things, and sometimes not even mention our kids. But then they would come up naturally in our conversation, without embarrassment or hesitation. We didn't dwell on their deaths but just matter-of-factly told stories or shared memories. Eventually we cried less. And we chuckled over the silliest things, like not remembering where the sentence we'd started was supposed to end. The first time I caught myself all-out laughing, I was amazed, thinking of how not that long before it seemed like something I would never do again. But now I felt freer, and it was all because of my new friend, Louise.

Once we were just sitting and not saying much of anything. It didn't matter that we weren't talking. I looked Louise straight in the eye. I saw all her grief, but I also saw strength, a will to go on. If my dear friend could do it, so could I.

"Louise?" I asked. "That day in the cemetery—why did you come up to me?"

"You were upset," she said.

"And you automatically wanted to help. That's just your way, isn't it?"

"Help?" Louise laughed. "You've got it all wrong, Martha. I was so sad I couldn't even help myself, let alone anyone else. I didn't have the strength to reach out. I don't know how I noticed your pain that day, I was so lost in mine."

At first I was surprised, but then I figured it out. You see, I'd been going to Restland nearly every day for months, but I'd never crossed paths with Louise. Until that day, just at the moment I needed her most. I believe God had seen me in my grief all along, and it was he who hit me with the overpowering urge that drove me straight to Louise, there beside Whispering Waters. He knew that we were meant to be together, that it was our own grief that could help us comfort each other.

Of course we both still feel the pang of loss. After all, the death of a child is like nothing else. But now, thirteen years later, autumn is again my favorite time of year. I stopped seeing it as the season of death, once I realized it was also the time when God helped me come back to life. He sent me an angel, a perfect friend. Louise, whom I met by the Whispering Waters. We are friends to this day.

To feel sorry for the needy is not the mark of a Christian—
to help them is.
—FRANK A. CLARK

A FATHER'S CARE

PAMELA KENNEDY

On a rainy Sunday morning, I put the coffee on and dashed out to the mailbox to retrieve the paper. As I neared the end of our driveway, I saw a young woman standing at the side of the road. She looked at me for a moment, then came closer. I could see she had been crying.

"Are you all right?" I asked.

She looked back down the road, then answered quietly, "Yeah, I guess. Could I use your phone?"

"Sure, come on." I motioned for her to follow me. When we entered the house, I answered my husband's puzzled look with a shrug of my shoulders. "She just wants to use the phone," I said.

I fixed our guest a cup of coffee and busied myself around the kitchen as she made her calls. In the next hour I learned quite a bit about our Sunday morning visitor. She was twenty-seven, a single mother who lived in a women's shelter in a neighboring city while her toddler son was in the custody of Children's Protective Services. "Lovey," who smelled like she had spent the night drowning her sorrows in a bottle, had taken a bus to our neighborhood in an effort to track down her child's father. She suspected he was seeing another woman.

"I just love him so much," she tearfully told me between calls, "but if I find he's been cheating on me, I don't know what I'll do."

I looked at her, sipping coffee in my cozy kitchen, and thought how easy it is to escape the world behind chintz curtains and scented candles until someone like Lovey comes along and gives a face to the sorrow around us.

And then I recalled how God refused to turn his back on the world that Lovey inhabits; how he sent Jesus to reach and teach and touch people with broken lives and broken hearts. I felt so helpless. What could I say or do that wouldn't sound hypocritical? I have a warm house furnished with nice things, a husband who loves me, and children who are strong and healthy. In the end I just hugged her, and she wept against my shoulder, sobbing that she didn't know what to do next.

After she made her last call, I took her hand and gave her a small gift of money and a copy of the New Testament.

"Lovey, I don't have any answers to your problems," I said looking into her large, dark eyes. "Only God does. He knows how you feel, and he wants to help you, but you need to spend some time with him so he can talk to you. I'm going to pray for you every day, and I want you to ask the people at the shelter to put you in touch with a pastor. God wants to be a companion to you and a father to your little boy because he loves you more than you even love yourself."

My husband took Lovey to the bus station after that. She left our home but hasn't left my heart. I often pray for her and wonder about all the other Loveys in the world who need to know that their heavenly Father can fill the emptiness when those we love are gone. In our loneliness and grief, he reaches out to us, offering to be both parent and loving companion.

> *The race of mankind would perish did they cease to aid each other. We cannot exist without mutual help.*
>
> —SIR WALTER SCOTT

JED'S MIRACLE

LINDA FRANKLIN

I watched my eleven-year-old son, Jed, on the floor beside his bed, fitting together the pieces of a jigsaw puzzle. Even two years after the accident, it was still hard for me to look at the raised, uneven skin of his hands. His eyes lit up as he slipped the last country into place in the world map puzzle that Charlie had given him that day.

A mutual friend put us in touch with Charlie after we'd moved back home to Canada. He was a middle-aged mechanic from a nearby town who, like Jed, had survived severe burns. Unlike Jed, though, Charlie had lost dexterity in his hands because of the mine-shaft explosion that injured him and still needed a lot of physical therapy. Still, he was always upbeat, and I thought of him as a godsend for Jed.

"Look, it's done, Mom," Jed said. "I can't wait to show Charlie next time he visits."

"That's great, honey," I said, helping Jed climb under the bedcovers. I tucked him in, then reached for the Bible on his nightstand and read to him awhile. Then I took one of his hands in mine for our nightly prayer.

"Mommy, why can't we do miracles like the disciples did?" Jed asked. I stroked the taut, rough skin of his right palm. "I don't know, honey," I said. "I wish we could."

We said our prayer and I turned off his lamp and said good night. I went into the next room and settled into bed, but sleep evaded me. There wasn't a day that went by that I hadn't thanked God for sparing my son. Yet his terrible scars haunted me, made me yearn to go back and erase the day of Jed's accident. I could still picture the San Bernardino Mountains as clearly as if they were right outside the window. My husband, Jere, and I had moved with eight-year-old Jed to those California mountains to become caretakers of a small ranch. The day that would change our lives forever was only the third at our new home.

That morning, after Jere drove off to work, Jed and I ventured into the cold January morning to do some yard work. After lunch, we set to scrubbing out the cement fishpond in front of the house. The sun was setting and fog was coming in as we finished refilling the pond with fresh water.

"Time to get supper ready," I said to Jed. "Want to start the generator?"

Jed jumped up and ran to the power shed at the back of the house. He had always loved machines and had been so excited when Jere showed him how to work the generator.

As I stood at the kitchen sink washing my hands, I heard a strange "whump" as if something heavy had fallen. I hurried outside. "Mommy!" Jed was running toward me, literally trailing fire. His face looked like melted wax, his hands like they were spilling from his arms.

Terror flashed up the whole length of my body as I ran to meet him. Frantically I tore off his burning jacket. The zipper melted into my hands.

"Mommy, put me in the fishpond!" Jed said. I pulled him over to the pond and eased him into the cold water. My mind raced. *Where do we go? The ranger station. But Jere has the car.* I caught sight of the wheelbarrow. *I can push him to the ranger station in that. It's less than a mile. But I have to keep him warm.* The fire had already spread to the house. Smoke was seeping from the windows. I had to hurry. I darted toward the front door.

"Mommy, don't go in there!" Jed yelled.

I pulled my collar up over my face to block the smoke and ran in. I grabbed two pillows and Jere's down jacket and ran back outside. Dropping the pillows in the wheelbarrow, I pushed it to the pond. I wrapped my shivering son in the jacket and laid him in the wheelbarrow looking up at me. "It's going to be all right, Jed. I'm taking you up to the ranger station." His face had lost all color and was swelling fast. I forced myself to meet his eyes. I had to keep Jed conscious, to let him know I was going to take care of him.

I grasped the handles of the wheelbarrow, ignoring the pain of my burned hands. I started up the hill, wincing for Jed every time we hit a rock. *God, please get me up this hill,* I prayed silently. *Get me up this hill.* "We're almost there, Mommy," Jed said.

The wheelbarrow caught on a large rock and I stumbled to my knees. "Oh, God," I cried, "I need your strength. Please help me get up this hill!" I struggled to my feet and, with one final push, got to within sight of the ranger station.

"Somebody, please help!" I yelled.

A ranger came running. He lifted Jed out of the wheelbarrow and took him inside the station. We laid wet paper towels on Jed's face and hands while another ranger went to call an ambulance. "You made it here just in time," he told me when he returned. "We were about to close up for the weekend." I heard sirens, then Jere was there. He had been stopped on his way home by policemen and told about the accident. In moments, we heard a helicopter approaching. Paramedics whisked Jed out to the copter. It lifted off for the burn unit at San Bernardino County Medical Center just before the fog closed in completely.

By the time Jere and I got to the hospital, Jed had been stabilized. But he had third-degree burns on almost 40 percent of his body. Swathed in bandages, his head appeared twice its normal size. His hands were tied to metal bars above his head and surgically cut to ease the swelling. He was on a respirator. I felt Jere's arm supporting me as I stood there, overwhelmed with the desire to bear my son's pain for him. I curled my hands into fists, trying to sharpen the sting of my own minor burns, which had already been treated. *If only I could take his place,* I thought.

Over the following days, firemen reconstructed what had happened. We learned the explosion occurred when the hot water heater's pilot light ignited fumes from the gasoline Jed was pouring into the generator, some eight feet away.

Jed began intensive burn treatments. He was given strong medications, sometimes followed by terrible reactions.

Jed couldn't see because his eyes were swollen shut, couldn't speak because of the respirator. And I knew the medication couldn't possibly block the worst of the pain. But he never cried.

One morning, I sensed something was troubling Jed. "What's wrong?" I asked. He shrugged.

"Is it about me?" He nodded and held up one of his bandaged hands.

He's worried about my hands! I swallowed back a sob. "I'm fine, Jed, don't worry," I said. Then he gestured at his legs. "You'll be up and running before you know it," I promised. For the first time since the accident I saw a tear squeeze past a swollen eyelid.

A few days later, he was able to watch television. Then he was taken off the respirator. Jed then underwent three skin-grafting surgeries.

The surgery was a success, and the nurses on the ward raved about how great Jed's new hands looked. I went into his room, eager to hold my son's hands again for the first time since the accident. But when I saw them, I hesitated. They looked purple, blotchy, cold. These were not the hands I used to hold every night after I tucked him in.

The scars were so deep on his face, on these "new" hands—he didn't look like my Jed anymore. But in his eyes was the same expectant gaze he always had when showing me the tracks he'd made in the dirt with his Tonka trucks. Inside he was still my little boy. All at once I saw that if I couldn't accept that—couldn't accept his new hands—then Jed might not either. "They look wonderful, Jed," I made myself say. Then I reached out to touch one of them. It was warm! And as alive as Jed was. I carefully took his hand in mine and watched him drift off to sleep.

After five weeks in the hospital, Jed was discharged and we returned to Canada. Soon after, Charlie came to see Jed. As well as Jed had coped with his accident, it helped him to talk to someone who'd been through the same thing. Yet now, lying in bed, recalling my son's question about miracles, I thought about how much Jed must wish someone could give him back his hands.

"Mom?"

I went back into Jed's room and stood by his side. What I could do to help him?

"You know what I'd do if I could work a miracle?" he asked. "I'd give Charlie back his hands."

I stayed there thinking about Jed's miracle and holding his hand long after he fell asleep.

Kindness in words creates confidence. Kindness in thinking creates profoundness. Kindness in giving creates love.
—LAO TZU

THE STRANGE POWER OF COMPASSION

ARTHUR GORDON

Not long ago I attended a memorial service for a successful business leader. In a subdued atmosphere of mourning, various friends paid tribute to him. Finally a young black man arose. The other speakers had been assured and eloquent, but this one, obviously under great emotional stress, could barely speak at all. A deep hush fell as he struggled for words.

With tears streaming down his face, he told the gathering that when he was just an office boy, the industrialist had noticed him, encouraged him, paid for his education. "For a long time," the young man said, "I was no good to him or anyone else. I just failed and kept on failing. But he never gave up on me. And he never let me give up on myself."

When his voice faltered to a halt, people everywhere were weeping, not just for the leader who was gone, but for the sorrow of the follower who unashamedly had revealed so much of himself. When the service ended, I had the strange conviction that somehow all of us had been changed for the better.

Later I spoke of this to a friend, a psychiatrist, who also had been there. "Yes," he said thoughtfully, "it was amazing, wasn't it? But that's what compassion can do. It's the most healing of all human emotions. If we'd just let it, it could transform the world."

The truth is, this quality of compassion—the word means "to suffer with"—has been transforming the world, especially in the last century or two. It was the force that abolished slavery and put an end to child labor. It was the power that sent Florence Nightingale to the Crimea and Albert Schweitzer to Africa. Mobilized in the March of Dimes, it conquered polio. Without it there would be no Social Security, no Medicare, no ASPCA, no Red Cross. But the most remarkable thing about it is what it can do to—and for—the person who feels it deeply.

Or even for the person who feels it suddenly and momentarily. Years ago, with two other college students, I was traveling one spring vacation in Spain. In Málaga we stayed in a pension that was comfortable enough but strangely somber. The owner, who spoke English, had little to say. His wife, a tall, tragic-looking woman, always wore black and never smiled. In the living room an enormous grand piano stood silent. The little Spanish maid told us that the señora had been a concert pianist but that two years ago her only child had died. She hadn't touched the piano since.

One afternoon we three American youngsters visited a *bodega*, a wine cellar where sherry was stored. The affable proprietor urged us to sample various vintages, which we did—and we sang and danced all the way home. Back at the house, full of thoughtless gaiety, one of my friends sat down at the great piano and began to play, very badly, while we supported him at the top of our lungs.

Suddenly the maid rushed into the room, looking appalled. Behind her came the owner, hands outstretched in a pleading gesture. "No, no," he cried. "You mustn't!" At the same instant another door opened, and there stood the señora herself, dark, tragic eyes fixed on us. The music died. For an endless moment, all of us were frozen with dismay and embarrassment. Then suddenly this woman saw how miserable we were. She smiled, and great warmth and beauty came into her face. She walked to the piano, pushed my friend aside, sat down, and crashed out the thunderous opening chords of the triumphal march from *Aida*.

The maid hid her face in her hands. The husband burst into tears. The señora kept playing—magnificent, soaring music that filled the whole house, driving the grief and the shadows away. And young though I was, I knew that she was free! Free because she had felt pity for us, and the warmth of compassion had melted the ice around her heart.

Where does it come from, this capacity to feel another's pain? I remember once asking a wise, old minister about that most famous of all compassion stories, the parable of the good Samaritan. How did the Samaritan get that way, I wanted to know; what made him sensitive and responsive to the needs of the wounded man when the other travelers who saw that crumpled figure on the road to Jericho simply "passed on the other side"?

"I think," the old clergyman replied, "there were three things that made him the way he was, qualities latent in all of us if only we'd work harder to develop and strengthen them. The first was empathy, the imaginative projection of one's own consciousness into another being. When the Samaritan saw the bandits' victim lying there, he didn't merely observe him, he identified with him, he became a part of him.

"The second thing he had was courage, and he needed it because it takes courage to care—and to translate caring into action. The ones who passed by on the other side were afraid—afraid of anything strange or challenging, afraid of getting involved, afraid the robbers might come back. The Samaritan had the courage to push those fears aside.

"The third thing I'm sure he had was the habit of helping. Going to the aid of the man on the Jericho road was no isolated incident in the Samaritan's life. He did what he did because he was the kind of man he was—and he didn't get that way overnight. Through the years he had trained himself to respond affirmatively to other people's needs. How? In the same way that any of us can do it, not so much by drastic self-discipline or heroic sacrifice as the endless repetition of small effort.

"Those things may not seem to add up to much. But one day you may look around and discover that, to an astonishing degree, self has been pushed off its lonely and arrogant throne and, almost without knowing it, you have become a Samaritan yourself."

Empathy, courage, the habit of helping—perhaps the old minister was right. And perhaps there are still other qualities hidden in the deep tenderness that we call compassion. Whatever they are, we would do well to seek them in ourselves and encourage them in others, work harder at developing and strengthening them. Because without this quiet power there would be little hope for tomorrow.

One filled with joy preaches without preaching.
—MOTHER TERESA

FINAL MOMENTS

RACHEL NAOMI REMEN, M.D.

ying people have the power to heal the rest of us in unusual ways. Years afterwards, many people can remember what a dying person has said to them and carry it with them through their lives. . . .

The sayings and perspectives of a dying person are often woven into our fabric, changing us from then on, helping us to live better. I carry in this way the death of a woman who in life had never been a close friend. She was outspoken, and somewhat judgmental, and I had found her edge intimidating. Though I admired her work and we traveled in the same circles, I had always kept my distance. Even when I was told she had been diagnosed with cancer, I did not personally call but thought about her and kept in touch with her struggle by calling mutual friends. Our paths had been converging for many years, but I had not known this and so I was surprised when her husband called me to say that Mary was dying and wanted to see me. Uncertain of why she had called, I went.

The woman who welcomed me to her bedroom was no one I had met before. Thin and completely bald, obviously gravely ill, her beauty was magnetic. As gracious as a queen, she patted her bed, indicating that I was to climb in and sit. I remember the four hours that followed as one of the most intimate, strengthening, and healing times I have experienced. We spoke of illness and pain, and she said with simplicity that she was no longer suffering. We spoke of the complexity that had characterized her life and all of her relationships, both family and friends. We told each other jokes. At one point her husband joined us and we read Proverbs 31, A Virtuous Woman, together. It was a favorite of hers. Certain of the lines are with me still: "She layeth her hands to the spindle, and her hands hold the distaff." "She is not afraid of the snow for her household, for all her household are clothed with scarlet."

Part of our discussion turned around the power of this time of dying in a person's life. She had experienced a liberation from some lifelong limitations and self-doubts and felt that she could now reach others in ways not previously possible. She felt grateful for this and for the clarity of vision that seemed to allow her to release her habit of anger and judgment and see the beauty in others. She wondered why this gift had been given her at this time and if it was to be used in some way. I told her that I felt that if it was, she would be shown how to use it. As our time together ended I felt reluctant to go, as if I had been granted an audience with a high lama. But it was only Mary. Eventually she fell asleep in the middle of a sentence and I left.

A few days later, her husband called to say that she had gone into coma, and asked me if I wanted to come and say goodbye. Her house was very still and peaceful. Climbing the stairs to her bedroom, I had the sense of a holy silence that she had somehow drawn around her. Mary lay in her bed in a deep coma, breathing shallowly. I took her hand and sat with her for a while, thinking of our last conversation. Suddenly her eyes were open. They were as clear as a young child's and as honest. In the intensity of her gaze I felt naked, seen in all my particulars and incompleteness. Yet I did not feel embarrassed or even vulnerable. She looked at me in this way for a long while and then she smiled gently and said, "I love you." Closing her eyes, she slipped back into coma.

I have carried the moment with me as a sort of touchstone. Her husband tells me that many of the people who came to see her after she went into coma had experiences similar to mine. She had opened her eyes and met with them in the same singular way, delivering the same last message. In looking back on it, it was a pure moment of intimacy and the power of it is not easily describable. I think of it as a sort of null hypothesis. The null hypothesis is a research principle that applies only when one is studying universal laws and principles, forces that hold in all circumstances and at all times. It states that should one find only a single instance in which the law does not hold, the law itself has been invalidated.

There are laws of our inner world that bind each of us as firmly as gravity, beliefs we carry about ourselves and about life in general that we experience as true in all conditions and at all times. A feeling of personal unworthiness is one such inner law. One moment of unconditional love may call into question a lifetime of feeling unworthy and invalidate it.

Perhaps these final moments with me and the others were a time of healing for Mary as well. After years of anger and self-doubt, the words of Proverbs had finally become true for her. "She perceiveth that her merchandise is good, her candle goeth not out by night."

Walking with Angels

God sends us angels to remind us of His love for us.
—AUTHOR UNKNOWN

GOD PROMISES TO SEND HIS ANGELS

BILLY GRAHAM

At times in my life I have felt protected in a supernatural way. We have been promised, "For he will command his angels concerning you to guard you in all your ways" (Psalm 91:11).

We face dangers every day of which we are not aware. Often God intervenes on our behalf through the use of His angels. The Bible is full of the accounts of angels.

Evidence from the Bible, as well as personal experience, convinces us that guardian angels surround us at times and protect us. Many Christians can remember when a near car wreck, a severe accident, or a fierce temptation was averted in some unusual manner. Angels may bring unexpected blessings, like a check in the mail for the exact amount needed, or some food on the doorstep when the cupboards are empty.

Once when I was going through a dark period I prayed long and earnestly, but there was no answer. I felt as though God was indifferent and that I was all alone with my problem. It was what some would call "a dark night of the soul." I wrote my mother about the experience, and I will never forget her reply: "Son, there are many times when God withdraws to test your faith. He wants you to trust Him in the darkness. Now, Son, reach up by faith in the fog and you will find that His hand will be there." Relieved, I knelt by my bed and experienced an overwhelming sense of God's presence. Whether or not we sense and feel the presence of the Holy Spirit or one of the holy angels, by faith we are certain God will never leave us nor forsake us.

Hush, my dear, lie still and slumber!
Holy angels guard thy bed!
—ISAAC WATTS

FIRST EMBRACE

SHERRI DERRICK

The scent of gardenias wafted through the window as a breeze billowed back the curtains. I rocked my three-year-old daughter, Kenly, slowly in our La-Z-Boy. Such a simple thing, holding your daughter in your arms, feeling the softness of her skin on your own, the warmth of her breath on your neck. For me it was the most precious part of being a mother—something I could never get enough of.

Maybe it's because I didn't get to hold her in those first moments right after I gave birth, the moments when a mother longs to keep her connection to the life that has been growing inside her for so long. In my case, it wasn't long enough. Kenly was born three months premature in an emergency C-section, just two pounds, seven ounces, and fourteen and a half inches long. I got only a glimpse of her little body before the nurse whisked her away to be cared for by others. My husband, Rocky, held my hand as the doctor turned his attention to us. "We're going to put your daughter in an isolette—it's a protective bubble. Her immune system isn't fully developed. She'll also be on a respirator until her lungs grow to normal size. You'll be able to touch her, but only through an opening in the isolette, until she's out of the woods."

Dazed and drained, I tried to absorb what he was saying. It wasn't supposed to happen like this. I had read so many books about becoming a mother, sat in our great big La-Z-Boy recliner practicing the right way to hold my baby. Now it was like I too couldn't catch my breath, thinking of my daughter fighting to live in a world where even her mother's touch could be dangerous.

Later that day we were taken to visit Kenly in the Neonatal Intensive Care Unit. It was an open floor with a nurse's station in the center and dozens of babies in isolettes spaced a few feet apart. I was wheeled in on my hospital bed by one of the nurses so I could gaze at my sleeping daughter. Her head was the size of my fist, her face almost covered by the respirator mask. IVs were in her arms, which were no thicker than her daddy's thumb. Her little chest was concave and her skin nearly translucent. If only she were still safe inside me where she could become strong. Instead she lay in this plastic bubble where I could not even touch her cheek. "Mommy's right here, Kenly," I said. "I love you."

I barely left her side. Even after I was released from the hospital I spent the entire day on a chair beside her isolette, trying to see if she had gotten bigger, telling her about all the people who were praying for her or singing lullabies and hymns. Sometimes the nurses would let me hold the syringe for her feeding tube or let me help weigh her, so I could touch her for a moment. As soon as I got home each night, I called the nurse on duty to check on her one last time before falling into a fitful sleep.

Finally after two and a half weeks, the nurse laid Kenly gently in my arms. I longed to hug her tight but could only hold her tiny frame gingerly in my hands, like a china doll. I turned my face away so my tears would not fall on her, and the nurse soon returned Kenly to her isolette.

The windshield wipers labored against sheets of rain as Rocky and I drove home that night. "I hate to leave her too," he said, "but she's in the best of care."

"What about when she cries, not because she's hungry or wet, but because she just wants to be held? After everything she's been through, I wish I could give her at least that much."

But soon I wasn't even able to visit her as often as I wanted. I had to return to work at least part-time so I'd be able to take time off when Kenly came home. I made a tape of myself reading nursery rhymes, singing, telling family stories—so she'd be able to hear my voice even when I wasn't there. I stopped by to see her before work each day. In my office, sometimes I'd close my eyes a moment and imagine Kenly in my arms, looking at me, reaching up to touch my cheek. Each night I returned to her side. "When we get home, Kenly, I promise all we'll do is sit in the rocking chair and be together." I would carefully reach into the isolette, lay my hand on her chest and pray, *God, please keep my baby in your arms while I'm away. Let her never feel lonely or frightened. Give her strength. Help her grow.*

Two months after Kenly's birth her doctor gave us the news we'd been hoping for. "I think her lungs are almost strong enough so she can go home," he said. "But she's going to need a lot of care. She'll be on a food and medicine schedule every three hours, around the clock. Are you prepared for that?"

He didn't have to ask. I would've done anything to get Kenly home. After ten weeks of having to let strangers care for her, at last I could hold my daughter whenever I wanted. I kept her crib in our room and often she ended up in bed with us. It felt so good to be able to comfort her when she cried or to sit in the rocker and sing to her like I had when she was in the hospital.

That's just what I'd finished doing that spring afternoon last year. The air was thick with the scent of gardenias. I laid the book on the coffee table and cradled Kenly in my arms. "Are you cozy there, honey?" I asked her.

"Yes, Mommy."

I rocked back and forth a few times, humming a made-up tune. Kenly nestled in closer to me. "You're so soft, Mommy," she said, "just like the angels."

Angels? Had we read a book about angels lately? No.

"Which angels, honey?" I asked.

"You know, Mommy, the angels who held me when I was a baby," she said.

I stopped rocking and sat her up on my lap so she faced me. "You saw angels when you were a baby, honey?"

"Yes," she said. "They held me all the time. Sometimes they passed me around to each other. They were so pretty."

"Angels held you," I marveled. Then I hugged my daughter tight, turning my tear-streaked face away just as I had when I'd held her for the first time.

Hold her close in your arms, God, I had prayed. Now I felt his arms around us both, mother and child, who'd always been in the best of care.

*The very presence of an angel is a communication.
Even when an angel crosses our path in silence, God has said to
us, "I am here. I am present in your life."*
—TOBIAS PALMER

KELLY'S ANGEL

DEE FLEMING

My husband, Don, and I pulled into the high school parking lot that cold December afternoon. It had been twenty months since the shootings. Twenty months, and still I could hardly bear to look at that building.

Sometimes it seemed like only twenty minutes since the April day in 1999 when we waited with the hundreds of other frantic parents for our children to make their way through the cordon of police and emergency vehicles surrounding Columbine High School. Some of the kids came out crying, frightened, stunned. Some were rushed from the school in ambulances.

One teacher and twelve students, including our sixteen-year-old Kelly, did not come out. For a day and a half they remained where they had died while investigators pieced together an account of two teenage boys who had fallen into the grip of a terrible evil—the evil that seemed to me to hover still about the place where it happened.

Like most of the others, Kelly was killed in the library, crouching beneath a table as bullets ricocheted through the room. *Just inside those windows!* I thought as Don got out of the car. Right behind that curved steel-and-glass façade. It was too much to bear. I turned my head away, unable to look.

It had been weeks before the examination of the crime scene was complete and police let the families visit the site. It was important to me to see the place where Kelly had tried to hide. I needed to pray at the spot, outlined in white on the floor, to kneel where she died. But if I thought actually going to the library would ease its menace, I was wrong. The bullet-scarred walls, the splintered tabletops, a shattered computer screen—violence and hate were still palpable there.

We live just two blocks from the high school, and for a long time I could not even drive by it, taking long, bizarre detours for the simplest errands. But for Don's sake, and for our older daughter, Erin, I had to pick up my life again. And what helped most was remembering how Kelly loved angels.

From the time she was tiny, Kelly and I had shared a special affection for these messengers of God. I can still hear her piping little voice, at age three, reciting the verse on the little guardian angel card my mother had given her:

"Angel of God, my guardian dear
to whom his love commits me here,
ever this day be at my side
to light and guard,
to rule and guide."

Kelly loved that card. I'd often see it on her dresser top or catch sight of it with her schoolbooks. When she was older we would sit together on the sofa and watch *Touched by an Angel*. We never missed an episode. We bought the soundtrack CD, too, and would sing along in the car, just the two of us.

For Kelly and me, angels were our shorthand for "God is near!" And his nearness is what made her such a happy child—a girl who woke in the morning with a smile and literally skipped through the day, blue eyes sparkling, long blonde hair swishing behind her.

That's what gave the library its peculiar horror for me. Kelly was such a gentle, trusting little soul to die amid such evil! I'd given her a poem about angels that she kept in a frame on her bedroom wall. After she died I'd step into her room again and again and read it, lingering over one line especially: "Angels are with you every step of the way and help you soar with amazing grace." I wanted to believe an angel had been beside her that day, with her beneath that table, helping her soar above the terror.

Almost as though they knew I needed them, people sent angel figurines along with their condolences. They came from friends, neighbors, total strangers—china angels, metal angels, wooden angels. An eight-year-old daughter of a friend tried to count the angel images in our house one day and gave up at 175—and every one of those angels whispered to me that Kelly was fine.

Only around the library was I unable to feel comfort. Not that we hadn't tried to exorcise the evil from that place. The school district at first wanted to repair and refurbish the space, but Don and I and the other parents believed that no child should ever again be asked to study there. God brought us together in an organization we called HOPE—Healing of People Everywhere—to raise money for a brand-new library building.

What began as a fund-raising effort among the families was caught up by the whole community, then by the entire nation and even beyond. The new school building was under construction now—Don had driven in that afternoon, as he often did, to check on its progress. "I'll stay in the car," I told him. I'd visited the building site with the other families just a few days earlier.

The new library posed no terrors. It seemed to me a sign of life continuing, life affirmed. It was the presence of the old site that continued to oppress and upset me. I glanced reluctantly at it through the car window.

Its exterior was unchanged, but inside, I knew, nothing was left of the old facility. Architects had come up with a design that preserved the cafeteria on the ground floor, while entirely removing the second floor where the library had been.

The cafeteria now had a spacious atrium feel, bright and light, with a beautiful mural of trees on the high ceiling, drawing the eye upward. Students and faculty of Columbine High School had a space that all could enter without fear. With the other families, we'd seen to it that no physical trace of the tragedy remained.

Yet for me, the place still threatened. I turned my back on it and stared the other way out the car window. *I need to know that Kelly's all right, Lord,* I prayed. *I need to know she's happy and at peace.*

Turn around. Look at the building. The nudge didn't come from me. That building was the last thing in the world I wanted to look at. I wrenched my head around . . . and blinked in astonishment.

Something bright was moving across those upper windows! Something shimmering and glowing, gliding slowly past the glass exactly where the old library had been. Open-mouthed I stared while the unmistakable figure of an angel hovered over that second story. Wings, radiant hair, flowing garment—no artist could have rendered a heavenly messenger of comfort more gloriously.

I sat awestruck, seeing, yet scarcely believing. *Even here, even here! Your angel was here with Kelly, just as you are with her always and forever.*

How long did the vision last—fifteen seconds? However brief the time on a clock, I knew the angel had given me a lifetime of assurance. In the midst of all the evil that ever was and ever will be, God is present. God is with us. God is stronger.

How many angels are there?
One—who transforms our life—is plenty.
—TRADITIONAL

IN THE PALM OF HIS HAND

T. SUZANNE ELLER

A first noticed it as I lay on the hard mattress of the cot at the kids' camp where I was a counselor. There was a small lump in my chest. And like the Princess and the Pea, I couldn't quite get comfortable enough to fall asleep. Many things crossed my mind as I tossed and turned through the night—my children; my work; Richard, my husband; and my homework from night school—but never did I think of cancer.

I was only thirty-one. I'd just skated through a physical six months ago. I felt busy, happy, fit.

So during the next few weeks I did what a lot of women might do: I put the discomfort out of my mind and pushed through my long days. Not only was I a working mother with three young kids, but I also taught Sunday school, was a youth sponsor, and took courses at the local college.

Who wouldn't feel tired? *A good weekend's sleep,* I thought, *that's all I need.* Yet exhaustion continued to shroud me as the weeks passed.

Finally, after two months of this lethargy, I called for another checkup. I lay on the hard, paper-covered mat of my doctor's examining table. He probed the lump in my chest, frowning. "How long have you known about this?"

"Two, three months," I said.

"I'm afraid it could be serious."

The next thing I knew a stream of nurses and technicians ushered me through a dizzying barrage of tests. My doctor returned with a surgeon to explain the situation to me, the two of them using a nightmare's list of words—*biopsy, oncologist, radiation, mastectomy, metastasized.* I was scheduled for surgery the next morning, they told me, and I should pack slippers and nightwear and try to sleep as well as I could tonight.

"No," I said, "don't schedule anything. I need to talk with my husband first. I need to tell my children. I need to arrange—"

"You shouldn't wait any longer," my doctor interrupted.

"Can you leave the room?" I burst out. "Please, I just need a minute alone."

As the door closed behind them and the room grew quiet and still, I bowed my head and clasped my hands. "God, I need you now more than ever," I whispered. "I'm in a tough place again, but this time, it is so very different."

Years before, I had bowed my head like this. I sat in church and heard the preacher drone on and on about God's love. A defiant and rebellious fourteen-year-old, I sat in that hardwood pew and narrowed my eyes. "I don't think you're real, God, because you definitely don't live at my house. In my house, my mother is struggling to make it from day to day. My older sister is hurting and running wild. In my house, my younger sister and brother and I have to stick together, because we're the only sure thing in our lives."

With all the ache and anger I had walled up inside, I said, "So if you're real, let me know. Now."

In the stained-glass dimness of the church I felt a warm light overwhelm me. In that one moment, everything changed. Every wall inside of me washed away. As the faraway voice of the preacher sang the wonder of God's love, I felt buoyed in the palm of his hand. Where I had been angry and hard and hurt, I felt suddenly forgiving and peaceful. Where I had expected nothing, I received everything.

By the time my doctor knocked at the door, I had regained some of the comfort of having God under me, some of the strength I had drawn upon for the last seventeen years. "Tomorrow will be fine," I said, "for surgery."

The next morning we explained the situation to the kids. My nine-year-old put her arms around me. "Mom, the doctors said I would never run, remember?" She kicked up her tennis shoes. In spite of being born with severe bilateral clubfoot, she played soccer and basketball and ran track. "Doctors don't know everything," she said.

But my doctor was right to move fast. That day's biopsy showed cancer. Two days later, I went in for a partial mastectomy. After the operation I read from the Bible on my nightstand and felt peaceful, but every person in a white coat carried bad news into my room. The cancer had spread. Several lymph nodes were positive. Then my doctor came in to tell us that the CAT scan showed a spot on my brain.

The air went thin in the room.

"If the spot is cancer, you have a ten percent chance of surviving the next five years—after surgery and treatment," he told me. "The surgery would be invasive and could affect your memory, your vision, your speech. We'll take an MRI tomorrow morning and go immediately from the results. I'm sorry."

I might die. What would that mean to my family? I didn't want them to suffer. I agonized over the thought of my children having to watch me grow frail, of their having to care for me. I began to lay out my wishes in detail to Richard, in case I came out of the surgery altered or didn't come out at all.

Richard picked the Bible up off the nightstand, his hand kneading the leather. "Stop," he said. "Don't talk like that."

"Listen to me, Richard."

"No," he said, "you listen—I don't want you to talk anymore, please."

He opened the pages to Corinthians and read: "But we have this treasure in earthen vessels, that the excellency of the power may be of God, and not of us." I knew the passage and heard his voice grow far away as the words washed over me: "We are troubled on every side, yet not distressed: we are perplexed, but not in despair; persecuted, but not forsaken; cast down, but not destroyed."

All the next day we waited for the MRI results, my room crowded with friends and family. My pastor led us in grace before lunch. Each time the door opened, everyone held stock-still. Then the door burst open. "It's gone!" my doctor shouted. "The spot's gone!"

The room erupted. My pastor leaped in the air. My mother-in-law beamed and clapped her hands. And Richard slumped against the wall and wept. My chance for survival had increased.

Later, my doctor told us that there was no explanation for a spot to have shown up on the CAT scan and not on the MRI. "I'm a man of science and not miracles," he said, shaking his head, "but I'd say you've been out of my hands since that first afternoon."

Two weeks later I sat in a chair and closed my eyes as the nurse administered my first dose of chemotherapy. I must have dozed off, because I could see myself lying there with the IV, Richard sitting beside me. Two others loomed tall behind me, one on each side, sort of hemming me in where I lay. Specialists, maybe? I couldn't see their faces, which were in shadow, but I knew by their stance that they were protecting me.

On the drive home I asked Richard who they were.

"It was just you and me, Suzie, and a nurse in and out to check on things."

"No one else? You're sure?"

"Positive."

We came home, made dinner, and played volleyball in the backyard with the kids. After we put them to bed, my mother-in-law phoned to see how my treatment had gone. "How do you feel?" she asked.

"It's unbelievable," I said, "but I feel great!"

"Well, I asked God to send you my guardian angel this afternoon. I wanted you to have two. You needed them both in that room."

The image of those two figures came back to me, and the hair on my arms and neck went electric. "I saw them," I said, shaking as I told her. God was not only real, he was present, holding me and my family in his unwavering hands.

To this day, I still shiver when I consider my progress. Beyond all understanding, I felt good enough to go back to work two weeks after the operation. During the long months of treatment, I never once felt like a cancer patient with a less than forty percent chance of survival. No matter what happened, no matter what my illness held in store for me, I could never doubt those sure hands. It's as if I stood, day after day, with my head bowed and my own hands cupped in front of me, expecting nothing, yet receiving, as always, everything.

Behold, I send an Angel before thee,
to keep thee in the way.
—Exodus 23:20

SOMETHING TO KEEP US CLOSE

LORI ONCINA

Well, Weewah, this is it," my father would say. "Weewah" was as close as I had come to saying "Lori" during my baby-talk stage, and my father had used it since. Squinting through the midday glare into my eyes, he'd rub my hands between his. "I'll be back before you know it."

Not yet five, I couldn't understand why my father, a baker by trade, had accepted a better-paying job as a long-haul truck driver. I didn't realize how much we needed the money.

As the days passed, I waited patiently, flipping through picture books of horses. Daddy had been a cowboy in his youth, and our passion for horses was just one of the threads that wove us together.

The moment I heard my father's truck pull in and the air brakes let out a big, steamy sigh, I flew through the door. He jumped down from the cab then whinnied and neighed like a wild horse—my cue to don my red Annie Oakley costume and meet him in the living room. I dressed in my cowgirl best, complete with white nylon anklets, scarlet boots, and shiny silver spurs. When Daddy got down on all fours I slipped the makeshift yarn bridle over his head.

"Giddyap, horsey!" I shouted between giggles and digs at his ribs. My father galloped around, dodging the furniture. He bucked and reared, trotting several laps around the kitchen and dining room. When his knees gave way, we collapsed in the middle of the floor.

Before one trip Daddy offered me an old laundered hankie. He rubbed it against his face and neck so it would smell like him. "Tuck it under your pillow," he told me, "close to your dreams." I fell asleep wondering what to give Daddy as a keepsake in return.

The next morning I knew: the white nylon anklets to my Annie Oakley costume! They were soft, small, and easy to pack. That afternoon I sewed them together the best way I could. When I finished, the socks looked like a white ball, and when I tugged they stayed securely together.

Daddy looked curious when I put the clump of shiny material in his hands. He studied it, then laughed, then cried.

The sock bundle found its place in his black leather shaving kit. Whenever he came home I washed the socks with lilac soap before tucking them between his shaving brush and razor. "God, please keep Daddy safe," I'd pray as I zipped the bag.

I grew up treasuring the gifts and trinkets Dad brought back for me from his trips. Even after I married and started my own family, he brought me a set of redwood squirrel lapel pins, ceramic ballerinas, pieces of CorningWare. When he turned sixty-five, Dad retired from the road. He and Mom divorced, the many miles of the road coming between them, and Dad moved into a trailer nearby. We saw each other often. If I didn't stop to visit, I still got a warm feeling just knowing he was inside when I passed by.

Several years after, I began to have what I could only describe as unusual feelings. Feelings of intense emotion. A sensation that I was not alone even when no one was around. I felt a presence with me, not standing behind or next to me, but almost standing in me, making me stronger. Stronger for what, I didn't know.

One morning as I drove by my father's trailer, the song "Leader of the Band," about a father passing away, came on the radio. I began to sob and had to pull to the side of the road. "No, Daddy, no!" I screamed. "You can't die!" I asked God not to let that happen. When the song ended, I pulled myself together as quickly as I had fallen under its spell. I phoned Dad as soon as I could. He was fine, healthy.

Strangely I was comforted when the next day, and every day that week, the same song played as I drove by my father's. Each time I sensed a powerful and reassuring presence with me. I cried, but the panic I'd felt the first time I'd heard the song was gone.

The telephone woke me in the middle of the night two days later. It was a nurse calling from the hospital. Dad had suffered a minor heart attack. I raced to the hospital. He was scheduled to have surgery in a few days and in the meantime he needed his rest.

I didn't leave his side until he asked me to bring him some warm socks from home. I picked up a couple of pairs from the trailer and returned to the hospital.

"Well, if it isn't the sock girl!" my father exclaimed to his roommate as I peeked in.

"Here they are, Dad," I said, unfolding a pair for him.

"You know, Ed," he began, "when Lori here was barely more than a toddler she sewed a pair of her socks together for me to take on the road. Those socks musta traveled a couple million miles."

"You remember those socks, Dad?"

"Of course I do. Can't say I remember where they are right now, but I know I still have 'em."

Imagine that. He still had those socks.

The next day right before his surgery, I squeezed my father's hand. "I'll be okay, Weewah," he reassured me. But he wasn't. Dad never woke up from the surgery.

After extensive medical tests and weeks of heartbreaking discussions, our family chose to have my father removed from life support.

I wanted to die right there with him. The same hollowness I had carried in my chest as a child, when Daddy worked a long haul, returned. Only now it was much worse. *God, help me stop hurting.*

When the time came for me to give the eulogy for my father, I walked shakily to the front of the chapel and gripped the sides of the podium. How would I get the words out? I took a deep breath and felt a strong slap on my back. I knew someone was with me again, helping me deliver the hardest words of my life.

The funeral over, I was left with the task of settling Dad's estate. I set about organizing the trailer, hoping in the process to discover a will or note or some indication of how my father had wished his possessions divided. After weeks of emptying drawers, turning out pockets and sorting through files, no will surfaced. Several times I was haunted by the feeling that I was missing something. After an exhausting month of searching the trailer, I arranged a casual get-together for the relatives to divide his belongings.

That day I went home to rest before going back to the trailer, where I had spent so much of the past few weeks. I couldn't remember the last time I had just sat down and done nothing since my father's heart attack. All of a sudden, an urgent need to return to the trailer seized me. Before I could question it, I was jiggling my key in the lock.

"All right, God," I said, "I know you brought me here, and I know you have your reasons. I'm tired. Please show me what I couldn't see before." And the thought came to me immediately, almost as if in response: *What about the burgundy suitcase?*

I'd sorted through it already. Nevertheless, I rushed to the utility room and pulled it from the shelf. I threw back the lid and instinctively dug deep into the back pocket. The same back pocket I had cleaned out twice, where I had discovered my father's lemon-yellow, Hawaiian-style shorts and a birthday card I had given him as a teenager. I thought the pocket had been emptied, but now my hand brushed something soft. My heart pounded as my hand emerged holding a little white ball. My white nylon Annie Oakley anklets! I buried my nose in the fabric and inhaled. Not lilac soap or diesel fuel: The socks smelled just like Dad's collar where I had buried my face for hugs.

I was more awestruck than surprised. God had been preparing me all along. He had sent an angel I could not see but whose presence I felt, a presence that gave me strength and comfort. The angel had guided me to an old suitcase. Inside was a reminder of how my love had traveled with Dad when I was a little girl missing him, how close we were even when we were far apart. As I held the socks I felt near to him again. He would not be returning from this journey, but we would always be together, held close by love.

*Whenever you are in need of anything, or are
facing difficulties . . . invoke your Guardian Angel.*
—Josemaría Escrivá

Dad's Untold Story

Barbara Shoemaker

My children were grown before I ever heard my dad, Howard, tell this story. He thought no one would believe him.

❦

Lots of hands were needed that June day in 1914 to clear the stony land for planting. Just five years old, I tugged at my father's sleeve. "I'm growed up," I begged. "I'm big enough to pick up rocks." My father couldn't deny my pleading eyes.

"Okay, son," he said. "Be careful. Stay out of the way of the mules and the wagon."

I was ecstatic. I tried to match my father's long strides as we walked to the barn. "Help me with the harness," my father said. I gripped the leather straps while he hitched up the mules to the old wagon. I rode proudly in the front next to my father. *Yes,* I decided as we bumped along, *I'm all growed up!*

When we reached the field that was to be cleared, I jumped eagerly from the wagon. "Careful now," my father said. "Stay clear of the mules and the wagon."

Rocks dotted the field. My brothers and I picked them up and threw them into the wagon. Once an area was cleared, the boys slapped the mules with the reins and moved the wagon forward.

"Let's see who can get the most rocks today!" my oldest brother, Martin, teased, and the boys laughed. I grunted with the weight of each stone I tossed into the wagon, but I wasn't going to let my brothers get the best of me.

We moved slowly across the field. Late in the day, after working a while in one spot, Martin called, "Let's go!"

But I spotted a rock under the wagon, beside the back wheel. *I'll show them.* I dropped to the ground. I crawled under the wagon and struggled to free the stone. I heard the slap of the reins and screamed as the rock-filled wagon rolled over my chest.

Suddenly an angel was there beside me. An angel, there in that rocky field. He reached out his hand, and I held it tight. He didn't let go.

"Howard!" my father yelled, scooping me up. Cradling me in his arms, he climbed into the wagon, and the others jumped on. All were quiet until we reached the house. Father ran inside with me in his arms, while Martin raced into town to get the doctor. "There's nothing I can do," the doctor said after examining the me. "I don't think he's going to live."

I lay in bed in my family's farmhouse. I saw the pain on my parents' faces, but I didn't remember the pain of the accident. No one realized I had heard what the doctor said. Yet I wasn't afraid because the angel kept holding me close. I recovered, but I decided to keep my angel a secret. Who would believe such a story from a child of five?

In 1979 Dad was diagnosed with cancer. As the end drew near, his mind went back to that June day in 1914. "A lifetime ago," Dad said in one of our last conversations, "and yet it's the most vivid memory I have. Will my angel come for me again?" We both knew the answer. All of Dad's stories are vivid in my own memory, but none more so than this one. I felt almost as if I'd seen the angel come for Dad myself. His secret sustains me, and forever will.

The guardian angels of life sometimes fly so high as to be beyond our sight, but they are always looking down upon us.
—JEAN PAUL RICHTER

A LADY WITH WINGS

CHRISTI MARIE

This is a new recipe," my grandmother said, setting a pan of pastry down on the table in front of me and my great-aunt Gertie. "Tell me what you think." At eighty, my grandmother, Loretta "Rita" Shultz, was as fearless as ever, always trying new things. I wished I had her confidence. "Tell me again about that time you got lost in the woods, Gram," I said while she dished out our dessert.

Gram and Aunt Gertie shared a conspiratorial smile. I'd heard the story a million times, but how they loved to tell it. "Well," said Gram, settling into her chair. "It was 1923 . . ."

"Late summer," said Gertie.

Gram nodded. "The corn was almost ready for harvest. Gertie and our sister Elizabeth went to get the cows back into the barn for the night. Even though I was two years old and not allowed to go, I followed right behind my older sisters anyway."

"We didn't know she was tagging along," said Gertie, who was only five herself at the time. "When the cows were back in the barn, Elizabeth and I washed up for supper. We all sat down at the table—even baby Tony was in his high chair, but little Rita wasn't there."

"Has anyone seen Rita?" her Mom asked.

"We shook our heads," said Gertie. "Then everybody jumped up from the table and started hunting everywhere for Rita. Mom called the neighbors and Dad searched the barns. When no one could find her we realized that Rita had to be out alone in the woods."

Gram finished a bite of pastry and sipped her tea, drawing out the story. "I couldn't see Elizabeth and Gertie ahead of me in the tall grass, so when they headed down the lane I kept walking straight into the woods thinking that I was following along behind them," she said. "But I wasn't, and I got lost. I hollered for my mother, but no one answered."

I closed my eyes and tried to picture my unstoppable grandmother as a toddler stumbling through the trees, cold and lost. "Worn out from walking so far," Gram continued, "I finally lay down behind a log and cried myself to sleep."

"We cried all night back at home," Gertie said. "Dad came to tell Mom they had closed all the coal mines so the miners could form a search party. The miners marched through the woods beside the farmers, so close that their hands almost touched each other, beating the bushes and tall grass."

"A priest came to sit with Mom in the kitchen to comfort her. He lit a candle, and we all prayed for God to send Rita's guardian angel to stay with her until the men could find her," Gertie said.

"So what happened?" I asked, reaching for another piece of pastry.

"Early the next morning I woke up and heard someone calling my name," said Gram. "I stood up and brushed off my dress, which was quite dirty from sleeping on the ground. Mom didn't like it when I got my clothes dirty. Then, through the trees, I saw our neighbor Mr. Gray standing there. 'There she is!' he called out. Mr. Gray scooped me up and wrapped me in his warm coat. He carried me all the way home—

over a mile away—and up the back porch steps."

"It was about eight o'clock in the morning," Gertie said, picking up the tale. "Mom flew outside and grabbed up little Rita into her arms."

"She was so happy to see me," Gram broke in, "she didn't even scold me for following you, Gertie."

"All us kids clapped and cheered," said Gertie. "Mom sat Rita on her lap and held her close. She said, 'Rita, baby, weren't you scared?' Rita just shook her head and smiled."

Gram was smiling now just at the memory of it.

"No, I wasn't scared," she said. "A pretty lady with wings had stayed with me all night and kept me warm. I don't think she has ever left my side, not once through my whole life."

I guess that explained Gram's confidence. It was given to her by an angel.

The powers of hell will assail the dying Christian;
but his angel guardian will come to console him.
—ALPHONSUS LIGUORI

GABRIEL'S LIGHT

ADAM DEMASI

My little brother, Erik, was the kind of kid who loved projects. He built elaborate models out of Legos and borrowed our father's tools to make forts in the woods behind our house. At Christmastime my parents and I watched him set off, dragging a saw half his size through the snow. Hours later he would reemerge, pulling the scrawniest pine tree along behind him. It was just like Erik to choose a tree nobody else wanted.

Putting up the tree had always been his responsibility. I didn't even know exactly where we kept the decorations, and I wasn't in the mood to sort through the boxes in the cluttered attic that day. I wasn't in the Christmas spirit at all. Four months earlier, Erik had died of a brain tumor. My parents kept telling me that Erik had gone to a better place, where God was watching over him, but I was bitter. Where was God when my twelve-year-old brother was dying? Why didn't God watch over him then?

I pulled down a box and untied the twine binding on the lid. A construction paper card slid out. Even in the dim light of the attic I recognized Erik's drawing style. On the outside of the card was a crayoned Christmas tree topped with a star. Inside was a short inscription with two angels leaning over it, complete with yellow wings and halos. I brought the card to my parents.

"I've never seen this before," my mother said, passing the card over to my father. "Erik must have drawn these after he had his dream," he said.

"What dream?" I wanted to know. Mom ran her fingers over the card. "One night," she recalled, "when Erik was already very sick, he dreamed of angels. He said the angel Gabriel appeared at his bedside and cast a light, warm and bright, as bright as Dad's blowtorch. The light made Erik feel well again."

"He asked us not to say anything about the dream," my father added, "but it was a comfort to him right up until the moment he died." I remembered that moment. We had been standing by Erik's bed when he turned his eyes to us and said, "I see the light again. I love you, Mommy and Daddy. I love you, Adam."

The light, I realized. *Gabriel's light.* Erik must have seen the angels again. God was right there, watching over.

That night we dressed our store-bought tree with ornaments, Erik's Christmas card with crayon angels and inscription propped on the mantel above:

To my family.

Thank you for helping me through my difficult time.

Love, Eriky

I imagined my little brother among the bright angels in heaven, hard at work on his latest project. And Christmas felt a little more like Christmas again.

Make yourself familiar with the angels,
and behold them frequently in spirit;
for without being seen, they are present with you.
—St. Francis de Sales

You're Real!

RAE ANN NELSON

I was surrounded by friends and family that September morning. Mother had flown up from Florida, and my daughter Michelle and her husband had come from Virginia. Teenage Leigh Ann and eleven-year-old Ryan stood by my bedside. My husband, Dave, sat next to me, holding my hand. I managed a smile, grateful for those who had gathered in my hospital room and the ones I knew were praying for me. I believed God was with me too, but deep inside I was more scared than I'd ever been in my life. I was a patient in the brand-new Genesys Regional Medical Center in Grand Blanc, Michigan, about to undergo brain surgery.

Ten days earlier I'd collapsed, my right leg and arm suddenly paralyzed. I'd felt numbness in my leg a few times in the past year, and my doctor had diagnosed sciatica. But this was something a lot worse. I lay on the floor alone and afraid. *What's happening to me?* I listened to the robins singing in the pine grove in the front yard. I thought of the Christmas tree farm down the road. Dave and I had been married only five months, and we were looking forward to our first holiday together in our country house. He was a wonderful man, and the kids and I were more secure than we'd been for a long time. *Will I lose everything now?*

"Come on, Rae Ann," I told myself, "you have too much to live for." I mustered enough strength to pick up the phone. Dave was on a run in his truck, but I got through to Leigh Ann at her job. She drove me to the hospital, where I had tests and an MRI. Later that day Dave and I met with a neurosurgeon. My MRI scans were displayed on a lighted viewing screen, and a frighteningly large tumor glowed in my brain. I had to have surgery right away.

"This is where I'll operate," said Dr. Mokbel Chedid, drawing lines on a dummy head.

"God," I whispered, "my life is in your hands."

The growing tumor had pressed on the nerves in my brain, causing my seizures. Dr. Chedid prescribed an anticonvulsive medication during the days before the operation. It made me groggy. "We'll take care of you," Dave assured me.

He and the kids waited on me hand and foot, but they couldn't calm my anxiety about the operation. I took comfort in the promise of Hebrews 13:5: "I will never leave you nor forsake you." Even as a little girl I'd hoped God was always present in our lives. My illness in recent months had helped me believe it: I'd felt someone next to me whenever I had a seizure. One time, when Leigh Ann held on to me, I told her to move. "Someone's already on that side," I said.

Although I tried to hide it, my fear grew. I asked everyone I could think of to pray for me. One friend knew a woman who had recovered from an operation like mine. The woman visited me, bringing a poem that echoed the Bible verse I'd been meditating on. "You are never alone," the poem said.

Michelle read the poem aloud that morning as I was being readied for surgery. Family, friends, prayer, consoling words, my doctor's belief that the tumor was benign—everything possible had been done to reassure me. But the look in Dave's eyes before the aide wheeled me down the hall showed me he shared my worries. *Will we ever see each other again?*

I didn't feel the anesthesia take effect in the operating room, and the next thing I knew I was waking up. I blinked, trying to distinguish what I saw. A beautiful face hovered over me, and a firm hand held mine. I tried to focus. My ears were ringing, and I felt like I was spinning. My dizziness was like being tossed on a violent sea, and yet that face steadied me like an anchor. Her loving eyes seemed to look into my soul. "Your surgery was a miracle," she said. Then the grip on my hand let go. She was gone.

The next forty-eight hours in intensive care were the closest thing to hell I can imagine. Pain was held at bay with morphine, but the dizziness was overwhelming.

When the dizzy spells ended on the third day, I wanted to get up and walk around the room. The nurse seemed amazed. Soon after, I was discharged. At home the kids handled things before and after school. Dave cooked every meal. At first it was exhausting just to get out of bed, but within ten weeks I was strong enough to do a little Christmas shopping in town.

Dave and the kids were astounded by my progress. So was Dr. Chedid. "Your brain looks as if you never had surgery," he marveled. *It was a miracle,* I thought, remembering the mysterious words I'd heard. I'd never figured out who had held my hand right after the operation, and I hadn't talked about it with my family. But I couldn't get her out of my mind. Some days, when I wasn't feeling well, I'd decide she was just a figment of my imagination or the effect of the anesthetic. But when the sun was shining and robins sang in the pine trees, I thought, *She was my guardian angel.*

One day as I left Dr. Chedid's office after a checkup, I strolled through the hospital. Recognizing nurses who had cared for me, I offered my thanks once again. Of course, the face I longed to see was nowhere to be found. Maybe my secret idea was the correct one. When I was ill and then in surgery, an angel had been at my side.

I was about to leave when I saw her. That face! A woman stopped in the corridor, staring at me the same way I was studying her. Then we hurried toward each other and embraced. "You're real!" I exclaimed, tears filling my eyes.

"Oh, yes," she said, that wonderful face lighting up. "I'm glad to see you looking so well!" Grateful as I was to her, I couldn't help feeling disappointed it hadn't been a holy presence after all.

"I'm very well," I responded, smiling.

"It's a miracle, you know," she said.

Her name was Sheila Richter, and she was a critical care nurse educator at Genesys. She'd stopped by the operating room on the day of my surgery to observe Dr. Chedid at work. "I could see you were afraid, Rae Ann," she said, "and I decided to stay. I held your hand and talked to you."

"I felt you near me," I stammered.

"There's something more," Sheila continued. "It's hard to explain. I tried to tell the technicians, but they just made fun of me."

"Go on," I urged.

"I felt a presence in the OR."

"What do you mean?" I asked.

"You were blessed, Rae Ann," Sheila said quietly. "During the operation I saw angels—a cloud of angels above you."

For a moment I couldn't speak. "Somehow," I finally said, "I knew they were there."

Sheila and I have become friends. The robins return each spring to my front yard, greeting me with song. My family has celebrated three Christmases with trees from the farm down the road. I've had no complications since my surgery, and my most recent MRI indicated everything is normal. "You are never alone," says the poem I was given, which now hangs framed on my living room wall. The presence I'd hoped for since childhood is real.

Nature's Peace and Comfort

*"Joy in looking and comprehending
is nature's most beautiful gift."*
—ALBERT EINSTEIN

NATURE'S RESILIENCE

NORMAN VINCENT PEALE

At our place on Quaker Hill in Pawling, New York, which we call The Hill Farm, our family has learned much from wise old Mother Nature.

One lesson is how trees handle storms. They move with the wind as it mounts in intensity, not with fear of the tempest nor by resisting it. They just bend with it, and as the tumult and force of a line storm gale increases, the boiling of the leaves of the gigantic old maples seems as if the tree is laughing with glee in the knowledge that it can ride out the storm, which it always seems to do. Next morning the storm is over and the sun is out. The ground may be strewn with leaves and twigs and perhaps a branch or two, but the tree still stands and actually is stronger than ever, having wrestled with and overcome another storm in its long life.

This tells us something about how we human beings can also ride out our storms in life. Bend with the wind. Lean against it. Laugh with it. Rejoice in struggle. It makes you strong.

I like the way pine trees handle a big snowfall. The accumulating snows lie heavy on the supple branches, but those branches seldom break. They just yield gracefully to the extra weight of the snow. And in due course the pine tree's friends, the wind and the sun, either blow it off or melt it, and then the branches slowly come back to normal position—which isn't a bad technique for a person to learn!

And then I cannot fail to mention our cherished old apple tree. It must be at least a hundred years old. Once it was quite large for its species: perhaps three feet thick, with a wide spread of branches. But now the trunk has been reduced to a width of no more than three or four inches, and at its center is a large hole two feet long and eight inches wide. But even this reduced trunk sturdily holds up the spread of branches. The tree is in a spot protected from the main force of winds, but it gets its share of the wind, rain, ice, and snow in the changing seasons.

I marvel at this tree, for it is old and reduced in structure, its youth and the vigor of its prime gone. But it does not know that it is old and weakened. Every springtime it puts out its blossoms, as it always has done, and as a matter of fact it seems to outdo the younger trees, for its branches are overwhelmingly full of pinkish-white blooms, and it is a sight to behold.

Then come the apples. We never have sprayed this old tree, but even so the fruit is crisp and juicy, apart from a few worms. It puts out leaves in the spring, to blossom and to produce apples in the fall; and it just continues, with fidelity to its purpose in being, to do that despite age and decrepitude. So every year, spring and fall, I go and stand beneath its spreading branches and reverently salute the old tree as my teacher, saying to it, "Dear old apple tree, I am going to keep on doing my job and I hope to do it as well as you do yours."

As long as I live and own this place, that tree will never be cut down, unless some winter gale proves too strong for it. Then I will sadly yield it to time and the elements, but cherish it forever in memory.

If having a soul means being able to feel love and loyalty and gratitude, then animals are better off than a lot of humans.
—JAMES HERRIOT

WISE ANIMALS I HAVE KNOWN

ALAN DEVOE

If I live to be eighty and still greet the morning with a praise-like prayer, it will not be from anything I have read in books of philosophy. It will be because I knew animals.

They are very close, said Saint Francis, to the paternal heart of God. I think they must be. By instinct an animal puts infinite trust in life.

This morning at sunrise I watched Thomas, our cat, greet the new day. Thomas is now (in human terms) going on eighty. Every morning I share daybreak with him. It is great medicine. First there is his rush up the cellar stairs, lithe and springy as a tiger, from the place where he sleeps by the furnace. While I fix his food I watch him. He always begins with the ritual of str-etch-ing. Nothing trivial or hasty, mind you, but a leisurely, carefully relished luxury that does him as much good as a vaca-tion. Left front paw, right front paw, now both hind legs, now a long bend of the back . . . aaah! A brisk shake; the big, green eyes open wide; the ears perk up.

He dashes to the French window, rears up with forepaws on the glass, and peers out all quivering, tail twitching with excitement. Sunshine! Trees! Great heaven, there is a leaf blowing hop-skip across the lawn! Thomas has looked out through this same pane hundreds of mornings, but every time it is fresh and challenging and wonderful.

And so with breakfast. You'd think he had never seen this old chipped dish before. He pounces on his food like a man finding uranium. Then, when the last bit has been neatly licked from the plate, comes the ecstatic moment for going out to the new day.

Thomas never just goes through the doorway. (Animals don't take these moments lightly.) First he glides halfway through, then stands drinking in the sounds, scents, and sights out there. Another inch or two and he stands again. At last, very slowly, he slips over the threshold. If so much wonder were to hit Thomas all at once, he could hardly stand it.

Now he rushes to the middle of the lawn and there this octogenarian performs a riotous caper. He takes a flying jump at nothing in particular, then zigzags after nonexistent mice. He leaps in the air and claps his paws on invisible butterflies. Then some quick flip-flops, rolling over and over, all four paws waving. In a minute it is finished and he steps gravely off to his day's adventures.

What better lesson in living could one have? Here is joy in every moment, an awareness of the electric excitement of the earth and all that's in it. One further lesson from Thomas: when he sleeps, he sleeps. He curls up in a ball, puts one paw over the top of his head, and turns himself over to God.

All animals give themselves wholeheartedly to the joy of being. At dusk in my woods flying squirrels play aerial roller-coaster. I have seen an old fox batting a stick in absorbed rapture for half an hour. Children react thus simply to the world about them, before reason steps in to complicate their lives.

If animals can be said to have a philosophy, it is as simple as this: When Nature says, "I give you the glory of the senses and of awareness, and the splendor of earth," surrender yourself to these things, not worrying if it looks undignified to turn somersaults at eighty. When the word is "Fight!" pitch in and fight, not weighing hesitant thoughts about prudence.

"Rest," says your monitor. "Play." "Sleep." "Feed and breed and doze in God's green shade by the brookside," each in its season. Heed the voice and act. It is a simple philosophy. It holds the strength of the world.

Animals do not know worry.

An animal doesn't know what brotherhood means, but when it hears the call "Help!" it answers instinctively.

Not only do the wild things meet life in all its aspects wholeheartedly, they greet death the same way. "Sleep now, and rest," says Nature at the end.

In animals shines the trust that casts out fear.

Nature and peace are my shelter and companion.
—WAYNE KRAMER

DAD'S ORANGE TREE

SUSAN GLEASON

I guess I've always been a daddy's girl. Dad ran the only funeral home in our small Minnesota town. Maybe it came from spending so much time comforting other folks, but from skinned knees to high-school heartbreaks, he knew just what to do or say to make me feel better.

It was no different after I grew up and started a family of my own. Dad was more than a grandfather to my two sons. He gave them support and advice from the time they started walking until they left home. When I went through my divorce, Dad was right there to ease the terrible hurt of that as well.

In the wake of the breakup, I decided to spread my wings, so I took a job in Arizona. The move was exciting—terrifying too. I'd never lived so far from my family before. The house I bought had looked homey enough when the realtor showed it to me, but once I moved in it felt all wrong—too big for a divorced woman whose kids had grown up and moved out on their own.

Dad and Mom came to Arizona to spend the holidays with me. It was my first Christmas without snow. That seemed to suit Dad fine. "You just haven't done anything with the place yet," Dad said. "It'll be wonderful once you make it yours. And look at that yard! Plenty of room for some nice trees. Let's go find a nursery and see what they recommend."

We bought a baby palm tree, only two feet tall, and planted it in the backyard.

Stepping back and wiping the dirt from my hands, I realized Dad was right. The place felt a bit more like home now.

I took root and flourished in my new home, just like that little tree. Each Christmas, Mom took a picture of Dad and me standing beside it, then beneath its thick fronds. With each visit came more plants and trees—hibiscus bushes, Mexican fan palms, and arborvitae soon crowded right up to the patio window. "Have the roses bloomed yet?" Dad would ask on the phone. "Make sure you're giving them enough water." Far as I was from home, Dad was keeping an eye out for me, just like always.

Yuma County, where I live, is one of the biggest citrus producers in the country. Orange orchards line the roads in every direction, and summer nights are full of their sweet, tangy scent. "I don't know why it took me so long to get one of these," Dad said one visit, unloading a baby orange tree from the back of the car. "This is an Arizona sweet orange. Before long you'll be making fresh-squeezed orange juice every day."

"How's the new addition doing?" he asked a few weeks later. I almost didn't have the heart to tell him. The little tree he'd planted had dried up and died.

On next year's visit, Dad bought another orange tree, this time getting vitamins for the soil and advice on watering from the nursery. But once again, the leaves turned brown not long after he and Mom went home to Minnesota. Over the years, Dad planted six Arizona sweet orange trees in my yard. None of them lasted more than a few weeks.

"I can't understand what the problem is with my orange trees," he said one Christmas Eve as we drove past an orchard just a half mile from my house. "What am I doing wrong?"

"Don't worry, Dad," I told him. "There's always next year."

Dad bought yet another orange tree when he came to visit that December.

Together Dad and I dug a hole in a different part of the backyard and planted it, but Dad's heart wasn't in it. He'd just turned eighty and for the first time, his age was catching up with him. He got tired easily, especially working outside, and complained about the cold, even on warm days.

That year's orange tree went the way of all the rest. Before he and Mom had left for Minnesota, its branches had drooped and its leaves had withered. All life was clearly gone from it.

"I guess we should dig it up," I said. Dad agreed. But every day we found another excuse not to. I got home from work too late, or Dad was too tired. Mom and Dad drove off at the end of January, the sad little tree still in the ground.

Two weeks later, I got a phone call from Mom. "Susan," she said, her voice shaky, "your father is sick. Very sick. I think you need to come home." Dad had been diagnosed with granulocytic sarcoma, a rare and deadly cancer. It was at an advanced stage and he was fading fast, Mom said.

By the time I got to Minnesota, Dad was already in a coma. There was nothing I could do but sit by his bed in the hospital, holding his hand and praying through that long day and into the night. Dad passed away peacefully the next morning. This was heartbreak like I'd never known before. *Dad would have found just the right words to help me,* I thought, *like he always did.* The only person who could comfort me was gone.

I flew back to Arizona a few weeks after the funeral. But as soon as I walked through the door of my house, it felt as cold and lonely as it had the day I moved in. *Lord, who will comfort me now?* I asked.

I took my coffee out onto the back patio the next morning. The first thing my eye fell on was Dad's last orange tree. *It's time I dug that up,* I thought. But sad as it was, that little tree reminded me too much of Dad. I couldn't bring myself to uproot it, not yet.

Slowly, mercifully, the routines of daily life took over. Sometimes I'd notice a new blossom in the backyard and catch myself making a mental note to tell Dad about it. The pain would surge up again for a moment, but I got through it. Little by little, I was moving forward.

Then one warm May evening, I was planting some bulbs in a patch of the yard near Dad's orange tree. *It's really time I got rid of that,* I thought. *I'm ready.* I took Dad's shovel from the tool shed and went over to the tree. Just as I was about to begin digging, I noticed something straining toward the sun in the grass beside it. A thin, green sapling, less then a foot tall, but already sprouting tiny, pale-green leaves. Carefully, I took one of the leaves, rubbed it between my thumb and forefinger, and held it to my nose. The smell—so tangy, so distinct.

Dad was gone. But the comfort I needed was as close as the leaf in my hand.

Flowers grow out of dark moments.
—CORITA KENT

BUTTERFLY LADY OF SWINNEY SWITCH

BETHANY HOMEYER

*P*erhaps it was meant to be. For my son's funeral a photo of a monarch butterfly was chosen for the cover of the program. Michael had lost his life at eighteen in an auto accident, and in my grief I clung to the hope of that image: the butterfly rising triumphantly from the chrysalis. A symbol of Christ's own promise of life after death.

And yet, in the weeks after the funeral, I found little comfort or reassurance. I dragged myself through daily life—fixing dinner, doing the laundry, driving to the post office—and then sank into despair. The smallest thing would set me off: a vision of Michael running down the path through the garden or stooping to pick a caterpillar off a leaf, each memory a deep ache in my soul.

Michael was my "nature child." He'd bring home insects, presenting them to me as though they were trophies. I'd stand there admiring the ladybugs he held in his chubby hand. "Be careful," he'd say as I leaned close. "Don't hurt them." He might keep them in a shoe box for a day or so, but he always released them back to nature to be free. Once, after washing his overalls, I discovered a bunch of pill bugs in the pockets.

"Look!" I showed the bugs to Michael. "They survived the wash!" We marveled at the hardiness of God's creatures and let them go in the garden.

Now I kept asking God the impossible: Why couldn't Michael have survived the accident? Why couldn't he bring my son back to me?

The only thing that kept returning to me was the image of that butterfly—a golden monarch fluttering across a clear blue sky, alighting on a flower. In the months after Michael's death I found myself irresistibly drawn to information about butterflies. I read books, looked for courses I could take, spoke with lepidopterists. Was God sending me this passion to fill the hollow space in my heart?

There are tens of thousands of species of butterfly living on every continent of the globe. They fly by day, sleep at night, and come in a dazzling variety: The coppery queen lives on milkweed; the black-and-yellow giant swallowtail drinks citrus nectar; the gorgeous ebony-and-yellow mourning cloak feeds on wildflowers. In my studies I felt close to Michael. He would have been fascinated. Sometimes I glanced up from a book and thought he was there, reading over my shoulder. Sometimes I talked to him as if he were still with me.

In time I began to see the study of butterflies not so much as a way to escape my grief, but to embrace it—to honor Michael's memory by doing something he would have loved. *I'll raise butterflies,* I decided.

We had the perfect place, a lakeside garden in our temperate Texas climate. I had always been interested in organic gardening, and we had plenty of trees and shrubs to produce leaves that would feed the caterpillars. I contacted a breeder, bought some larvae, and put them in shoe-box-size containers lined with paper towels and leaves. Day by day I watched the caterpillars grow until they formed their chrysalides. Then came the moment when they slowly emerged and unfurled their wings. When they took flight, the sky above my garden was filled with color, as though flowers had taken to the air.

That first summer of raising butterflies brought one joy after another. I felt Michael near me, the way he had been at my side as we watched bees buzz from flower to flower. Released from my sorrow, I wanted to share this beauty with others.

I kept thinking about all the milestones that Michael would never reach—graduation from college, his wedding, the birth of his first child. And then I had an idea: Why couldn't I start a business offering butterflies for such occasions? To celebrate beauty, joy, and freedom. Michael's Fluttering Wings, I called it. He would have liked that. With the help of some friends, I launched the company.

Since we started Michael's Fluttering Wings five years ago, we have provided thousands of butterflies to fill the gardens and skies at countless events. We take great care of our butterflies, feeding them in their boxes and then keeping them in a large netted cage with plentiful nectar. I am incredibly thankful for this business, the way it lifted me out of my grief and showed me how to move from mourning Michael to honoring him. Yet it was not an overnight process.

Not long ago I was reading about an experiment done by the great English biologist Alfred Russel Wallace. Observing an emperor butterfly struggling to leave its chrysalis, he wondered what would happen if he helped the process along. He slit open the chrysalis with a knife. But, as he wrote, "The butterfly emerged, spread its wings, drooped perceptibly and died." Without the pain and intensity of the struggle to get free, Wallace concluded, the butterfly lacked the strength necessary to survive.

I thought of how I came through the grief of losing my son. It was a long, at times agonizing, struggle, and yet in it I found the strength to go on, to accept the wings God offered.

Nature teaches more than she preaches.
—JOHN BURROUGHS

LIFE'S EXTRAS

ARCHIBALD RUTLEDGE

A remember one October night visiting a friend who was lying very sick. There was a full moon that night; and as I walked down the village street on my sad mission I felt the silvery beauty of it quiet my heart. The world lay lustrous. . . . [My friend] felt the breeze, too, and delighted in the odors that it brought of the happy world beyond his window.

As I sat beside him, a mockingbird began to sing in the moonlight, chanting divinely. I know the song reached our spirits. On the table by the bed were all the necessities for a sick man; but he had small comfort from them. But the moonlight, and the hale fragrances, and the wild song of the bird—these brought peace to his heart.

Long afterward he said to me, "Do you remember that night? I thought it would be my last. But from the time the birdsong came through that window I felt that I would get well. I don't talk much about these things, but I felt that all that beauty and peace were really the love of God. I guess he does not love us with words: He loves us by giving us everything we need—in every way."

It must be as he said.

At any rate, I know that a thoughtful consideration of life's extras has done more to give my faith in God actual conviction than all the sermons I ever heard. My knowledge of theology is hardly ample; but I am absolutely unshaken in my faith that God created us, loves us, and wants us not only to be good but to be happy. He ministers to our bodies by the necessities that abound in the world, and to our spirits by the beauty that adorns creation. One has no difficulty in discovering, in the vast scheme of things, an extraordinary, an exciting, provision and prevision. As philosophy, I know not if this will stand; but I do know that a belief in it has brought me close to God.

I cannot regard the "fiery funeral of foliage old" as accidental, nor the gorgeous pageantry of sunset as anything but the manifestation of divine art. I stood recently on the shores of a mountain lake at sundown after a heavy rain, and watched for an hour the magnificence of the west: the huge clouds smoldering, the long lanes of emerald light between them, then isolated clouds like red roses climbing up some window of the sky, the deep refulgence behind it all. Superb as it was, momently it changed, so that I saw in reality a score of sunsets. I looked across the lonely, limpid lake, past the dark forest, far into the heart of the flaming, fading skies. I was sure that God had done that; moreover, that he had done it for a purpose. When did he ever do anything idly? And what was the purpose? Surely to fill the hearts of his children with a sense of beauty and of awe, and to teach them of his loving care.

Neither a day-dawning nor a sunset (with all its attendant beauty) is really a necessity. It is one of life's extras. It is a visit to an incomparable art gallery; and no one has to pay any admission fee. The human mind, being somewhat proud and perverse, may be inclined to reject this kind of proof of God's love. But the human heart can hardly do so. And in things spiritual I am sure that the heart is by far the better guide. . . .

I mentioned sunsets and sunrises as extras. Almost the whole complex and wonderful matter of color in the world seems an extra. The color of the sky might have been a dingy gray, or a painful yellow, or a plum-colored purple. But it is sapphire; and my philosophy makes me believe that such a color for the sky is by no means the result of mere chance. Granted, it is the result of the operation of certain laws, forces, and conditions; yet behind it all, back of the realized dream, is the mighty intelligence of the Creator, the vast amplitude of the dreamer's comprehension. And let us not forget that the two colors at which we can gaze longest are blue and green. There is about them a coolness, a serenity, a spirit of fragrant peace. And as the blue prevails in the sky, the green does upon the earth. . . .

I remember walking early one July morning down a thickety path. Trees completely overarched it, but far ahead light gleamed. The path was long and straight, and terminated in a wide meadow. As I glanced upward, my eye caught sight of what I supposed to be a knot on the end of a dead limb that hung directly over the pathway; it was clearly silhouetted against the sky line ahead. In a moment something had darted over my head and had alighted on the knot. It was a hummingbird on its nest, which hung like a fairy bassinet in the lonely woodland. I looked at the nest and at the bird, with its elfin grace, its delicate sheen of brilliance, its jeweled throat. And I thought: This whole matter of grace, of elegance, of delicacy and felicity of beauty is an extra. It is not necessary to have it so. But God has willed it so, because he loves us and knows our hungry hearts need this kind of beauty.

For many years, I had an idea that nature had for man an active sympathy; but now I have changed my opinion. There seems really a superb indifference about nature. It is what lies behind nature that really has sympathy. The rose does not of itself bloom for us; but God has made it to bloom for us. Surely this beauty is not a random affair; it is too authentically a sign and symbol of love. All we know about the highest form of affection we have learned directly from God's affection for us. We not only "love him because he first loved us," but we love one another because he teaches us how. We originate with him; and our sublimest art is nothing but attempts to imitate the things in nature that He has created.

Whatever my religion may be worth, I feel deeply that life's extras have given it to me; and time shall not take it from me. . . .

I am the light of the world: he that followeth me shall not walk in darkness, but shall have the light of life.

—JOHN 8:12

THE PAINTER OF LIGHT

THOMAS KINKADE

One afternoon, early in my career, I attended a showing of my work in a small gallery in northern California. Among the people who stopped by to see my paintings, there was a man who wandered in off the street, saw the brightly lit artwork (as well as the complimentary hors d'oeuvres!), and decided to stroll around the show. After making his rounds, he pulled up beside me.

"So," he said, "why does this Kinkade guy have all the lights on in his paintings?"

"I couldn't tell you," I confessed.

"Well, if you see him," said the man, "ask him for me."

In a sense, I have spent my career trying to answer that question.

When I was a child, I would come home after school and our house would often stand empty, dark, and cold. I'd hope, as I approached, that the lights would come on suddenly—that someone would swing open the door and wave and smile as I quickened my step.

I could hope, but I knew that no one would be home. My father had left us when I was little, so my mother worked late as a secretary to support the family. My brother and sisters frequently got home from school after I did. I would scuff my heels along the sidewalks beside shadowy hedges and sycamore trees. I would stop and study a bird's nest or some wildflowers or perhaps the way wood smoke curled out of chimneys on cool days, but mostly I'd look at all the other houses I passed, the lights on in their windows, the brightness so inviting I wanted to dash up and ring the bell and wait to be offered some cookies and warm cinnamon milk.

When I finally reached my house, I was hesitant to open the door and go in. It was more than just being afraid of the dark. The lights within other houses on our street filled me with longing. I wished the whole world could be lit up like those houses. Even as a latchkey kid, I was a bit of a romantic.

By no means would I describe my childhood as a miserable one. In the foothills of the California Sierras, in the small town of Placerville, we Kinkade children enjoyed a blessed upbringing. My brother and I made a tree house in our backyard and rolled go-carts down our drive. We would attend services at a country church down the lane from our house, the Kinkade clan taking up the length of a pew. I would sit mesmerized not by the voice from the pulpit, but by the blue glass windows overhead and flickering yellow lights of the candles at the altar.

After high school, I took all my romantic aspirations and small-town innocence with me to the University of California at Berkeley. I wanted to become an artist of the people, a communicator with paint, the next Norman Rockwell. I had a desire to touch people's lives with my paintings, and I believed that if I could be true to myself, if I could express my feelings and paint from my heart, my work would speak to people. Why else would I want to paint but to share the joy and light I felt inside with others?

Talk about culture shock! My homespun values were about to clash with twentieth-century intellectualism. No one at Berkeley seemed to find much merit in my idealistic approach. People were creating art around dark or pessimistic themes, exploring tortured inner feelings, childhood pain, and personal insecurities. My fellow students urged me to get in touch with inner demons. My paintings were deemed clichéd and sentimental and outdated.

I suppose I should be grateful for that period of my life, for the way my beliefs were tested. But at the time, each class hour felt like a blow to the stomach, my professors all fighting to tear down my idealism. To them, artwork was supposed to shock and disturb the viewer, not provide comfort and joy. In my dorm room at night, I would lie awake, plagued by doubts. I worried that my professors had it right, that my vision was naive and simplistic. The light began to fade from my dream.

By the end of the year, I gave up on the art program altogether and switched to the College of Liberal Arts, studying literature and humanities. With each spare hour I had, I painted alone in a basement studio and did illustrations for a local newspaper, but every day was a struggle to discover how I could ever become the painter I'd vowed to be.

I'd pray for counsel but didn't have any answer besides quietly painting and drawing and keeping my creative flame alive through work and hope. Then one day a friend asked me to a revival meeting and, to my surprise, I said yes. I was twenty-two years old and I'd not gone to church regularly since I'd left home. I remembered the lights and glass and burning candles of my hometown chapel. Maybe the smell of a church would lift my spirits.

But the auditorium was dark and uninviting, part of an abandoned college, and I wondered what good could come out of a place as dreary as this. With its faded drapes and dusty windows, I couldn't see the slightest promise of light in the place. As the enthusiastic young preacher's voice rose and his words, like a long-lost lifeblood, reached my heart, I felt something good within me stir. It was like the feeling I once got looking at a house all ablaze with the warmth of light, as if I at last had found home.

"God's in the room," the preacher was saying. "He's waiting to touch your life, to meet your every need, to fill your life with light. He's here. If you want to know him, come down to the altar. Come down to the altar now."

Without consciously willing it, I was suddenly rising and making my way down the aisle to the preacher, his words entering me like light enters glass. At the front of the auditorium, I found myself kneeling. *Open the doors,* I was praying. *Open the doors you want me to go through, God. I commit whatever talents I have to you. If there is any way you want to use me, please show me the direction clearly, dear God.*

I felt myself filled with what I'd always wanted to fill my canvases with, felt lifted out of the dark morass of confusion. I sensed a freedom I'd never known before, freedom to paint as I had always wanted to. And from that day, it has been my life's mission to fulfill that dream of light and bring it to people.

To convey hope and joy to others, the scenes I paint are alive with light. Each canvas is infused with brightness, because I believe this is how the world can be and sometimes is. A lighted window says home to me. It says all is well with the world, someone's waiting, someone cares.

Most of all, light exists in the dimension of the spirit. It was what God first created and is probably the most consistent metaphor in all of Scripture. Truth is represented as light, and in Matthew 5:16, Christ affirms that each of us should "Let your light so shine before men, that they may see your good works, and glorify your Father which is in heaven." But light is something you can't hold. You can't touch or taste or pin down its subtle, constantly changing effects. As a painter, light is the essence of what I try to capture on canvas—a light that dispels darkness, that chases away confusion and despair.

For me, the brightest light burns inwardly. With this supernatural, inspiring light, God illuminates our spiritual path and leads us to heaven through the love of his son. And heaven, at least in my artistic imagination, is a place where the windows always glow.

*When one tugs at a single thing in nature,
he finds it attached to the rest of the world.*
—JOHN MUIR

THERE'S A FLYING SQUIRREL IN MY COFFEE

BILL GOSS, LT. COMMANDER, USN (RET)

The doctor clears his throat, then tells me the three most dreaded words in the English language:

"You have cancer." . . . *You have cancer.*

Suddenly I feel like I've been dead asleep for centuries, only to be blasted awake in an instant to find myself treading water, alone, in the dark, in the vastness of the Pacific Ocean. I don't know when the sharks and barracudas are going to pull me under and shred me to ribbons, but I know there is no possibility of escape. A feeling of complete and total despair. Over the entire course of my thirty-eight years on earth, which has included many close calls, I have never felt so alone before. . . .

I put on my game face. After all, I was a brave Navy pilot. *Keep thinking positive,* I said to myself. . . .

A large amount of research has gone into the powerful bond that exists between humans and animals. Recently, a lot has been written about the subject, particularly by a great friend of mine in Idaho, Dr. Marty Becker, the veterinary contributor to ABC's *Good Morning America* and author of the bestseller *The Healing Power of Pets.* In my opinion,

Marty Becker has done more than any other person I know to prove that our greatest healers, teachers, and heroes have fur, feathers, and four legs. . . .

Besides my family and friends, one way that I tapped in to my love of nature and of all animals in a very large and meaningful way was simply by spending more time at the water's edge on our dock, our nature walk, and our pond and waterfall. You might say, "Well, we don't have a pond or a waterfall in our backyard." That's the point. Neither did we. So we saved our money and we dug a pond, and built a waterfall, nature walk, and dock. You don't always have to go to nature. You can bring nature to you. . . .

Dr. Rossi called soon after I got home from the hospital to tell me he had a favor to ask of me. It seemed that someone had brought to his office a tiny ball of fur that had fallen from a nest high above in an oak tree. And that ball of fur, about the size of a walnut, was alive. It was a baby flying squirrel, not yet weaned and just about to open its eyes. Dr. Rossi and his wife had nursed the little guy back to health. Now he needed a permanent home.

John felt that this tiny baby squirrel might be just the distraction—and just the medicine—that his sliced and diced, morphine-addled friend might need to help him through his cancer challenge. Dr. Rossi didn't share any of those thoughts with me at the time, nor did he share with me how many times he has had to put down his clients' favorite pets because of skin cancer and melanomas, a not uncommon disease, particularly among older dogs and cats.

"John—yeah, sure, a pet flying squirrel—yeah, that would be really fun," I said to him on the phone.

"We'll bring it over later this afternoon," he replied. "Bill, wait till you see this little guy. He's really cute. He's just opened up his eyes."

A few minutes later, jokingly, I asked Peggy and the kids if they minded if another aviator came to live with us. Peggy gave me a questioning look; my bachelor Navy pilot buddies were the last people on earth she'd want living with us full-time. Some of them tended to be, well, just a tad wild.

When I told her the houseguest I was proposing was a tiny flying squirrel and not a Navy pilot, she and the kids were delighted. Always the animal lover, and especially a sucker for cute and cuddly baby animals, Peggy helped me set up a tall white birdcage in our kitchen for the furry little aviator's arrival.

Soon, this tiny furball was nestled in the chest pocket of my burgundy terry bathrobe, munching on a pecan, a favorite treat. As he stared up at me from the pocket of my robe with his enormously out-of-proportion jet-black eyes, it was easy to see how the southern flying squirrel ended up with the Latin name *glaucomys*, which means "bulging eyes." . . .

The smallest of the North American tree squirrels even when full grown, this baby squirrel, just a few months old, with its silky gray-brown-fur back and pure-white-furred belly was a joy to behold. I instantly connected with this tiniest of creatures. And it appeared that the feeling was mutual. He fell asleep in my bathrobe pocket as soon as he finished the pecan Christie had given him.

"What should we name him?" Peggy exclaimed. "Rocky!" Brian and Christie immediately cried out. Peggy, not a fan of such simple and obvious names for pets, tried to argue against it, but the twins' delight in what they thought was the best and most original name imaginable won out in just a few short minutes. I was in no shape to argue with them, and Rocky seemed an easy name to remember. I needed things to be easy right then.

After about an hour, Rocky woke and scampered to the top of my head. He then peered down at my left ear as if to say, "Oh, boy, what happened to that?" He probably thought one of his larger cousins, a gray squirrel perhaps, had jumped out of a tree and chomped off my ear.

Rocky decided he liked it up on the top of my head, and almost every day he would sit up there, eat a pecan, and generally survey his squirreldom until he was ready for bed. At siesta time, Rocky sat on top of my scarred shoulder underneath my bathrobe or surrounded by fluffed-out cotton in the nest box in his cage, giving both of us a chance to catch up on some valuable time to reflect on our rather unique pasts. . . .

Over the course of the next few weeks, on a diet of nuts, fruits, mixed bird seed, and vegetables, Rocky grew from the size of a single walnut to the size of a bar of soap, about four or even six walnuts in size, collectively.

One morning, while I was reading the *Florida Times-Union* with Rocky perched on top of my head, busily grooming himself, I raised a cup of coffee to my lips with my right hand while I continued to hold the newspaper with my left. Peggy and the twins were running around the kitchen getting ready for school. Suddenly: "Ah-chooooo" I closed my eyes and sneezed with all my might. Nicely recovering from the sneeze, still holding my coffee with my right hand in front of my face, I again tilted the cup up against my lips. To my amazement, staring directly at me were Rocky's two huge eyes, now with his front little feet perched on the edge of the cup, as if he were kneeling in prayer, perhaps praying to get out of this unlikely predicament.

"There's a squirrel in my coffee!" I cried out in utter amazement to Peggy and the kids.

Like a flash, Rocky shot out of the cup and onto my shoulder, and then, with one more leap, up to the top of my head again. I could feel him preening himself, licking the coffee from his drenched fur like there was no tomorrow. What a caffeine buzz Rocky was going to get, I thought.

But then I had another thought, and it was this: Lately I had been feeling a bit sorry for myself. Maybe I was feeling a little bit of "Why me, God? Why did you give me cancer at only thirty-eight years of age? What did I do wrong? Wasn't I among your chosen—don't I count—aren't I one of your more unique creations?"

The answer was forthcoming, a truly profound realization for me, inspired by Rocky's dip in my coffee. God wanted me to know that of course I was unique. Because I absolutely, positively had to be the only person in the world—out of the six billion or more people walking the face of the earth at any given moment—who had a flying squirrel in his coffee that morning. [That] made me unique. [That] made me special.

And sometimes it is that feeling of being unique, of being special and one with God, particularly when you're reflecting on the immensity and infinite nature of the universe, that takes away the sense of aloneness, and of being separate and unconnected to the universe. Feeling unique can make all the difference in a person's outlook about getting well again. It can help to supercharge your human spirit, help to kick it into afterburner.

Especially for a guy like me, a Navy pilot, with a tiny little furball of an angel not yet qualified to fly, serving as my new copilot.

Hope is the thing with feathers, that perches in the soul.
—EMILY DICKINSON

INVISIBLE WINGS

ANN CULBREATH WATKINS

The summer of '92 wasn't easy for me, easy the way those slow hot months in Alabama should be. I'd just come out of a domestic violence shelter, where I'd taken refuge from an abusive relationship, and was trying to face the fact that I had to start my life over. My father had set me up in an old mobile home a stone's throw from his house, "so you can have some privacy while you get back on your feet," he'd said. Dad had done everything in his power to cheer me up, but it wasn't working. "I know just the thing," he said one day.

On a clothesline outside the trailer, Dad hung three plastic hummingbird feeders that had belonged to my mother before she died. I remembered them well from the summers of my childhood. *Will I ever be that happy again?* I wondered while Dad filled each feeder to the brim with sugar water. "Mother always used to say there's nothing like a hummingbird to take your mind off your troubles," he said. "A tried and true remedy." But troubles like I had didn't go away so easily.

"Thanks, Dad," I said, hugging him before he started home. I forced a smile when he looked back over his shoulder to make sure I was all right. I couldn't quite picture ever being all right again, and part of me wondered if I deserved to be. They'd told me at the shelter that a lot of women who'd been through what I had felt that way.

The next morning I stood in the doorway of the trailer. *Lord,* I asked, *what do I do now?* I moved outside and leaned up against a spot of shade on the aluminum siding. Just then a bright blue-green hummingbird buzzed one of the feeders. He lined up with the flower-shaped feeding port and took a sip through his long needle of a beak. His wings beat so fast they blurred to invisibility. The hummer looked like he was dangling in midair, like a spider dropped from an invisible thread, and hardly much bigger.

For a fleeting second Mother's hummingbird remedy worked: I was distracted from my worries. But how many hummingbirds would it take to truly lift my spirits?

I walked over to Dad's. "One already, huh?" he said when I told him about my first visitor. "That's a good sign."

Back at the trailer that afternoon, I was surprised to see a female hummer at the feeders. She was dressed in more modest colors but stunning nonetheless. Gracefully she zoomed up for a drink. Then a third hummer jostled for position at the same feeder.

By week's end I'd counted twenty hummingbirds! I took to sitting outside, watching them from a lawn chair just a few feet from the feeders. My presence didn't seem to bother the birds in the least. Every day, rain or shine, they buzzed the feeders. Evenings when Dad sat with me, the tiny creatures flew round his red cap.

One of the females, drab in color but with a beautiful calm air about her, became my steady companion. While I sipped coffee in my lawn chair one morning, she perched on a bit of clothesline above my head and preened her feathers. *I should take good care of myself too,* I decided. I relaxed in a cool shower, spent a little extra time on my hair, and arranged a big wildflower bouquet for the kitchenette. By day's end I felt a sense of hopefulness tiptoe into my heart. Maybe, just maybe, I was going to be okay.

When the director of the shelter telephoned to check on me a couple weeks later, she commented on the change in my voice. "You're finding your wings," she said.

As we talked, a hummingbird zipped inside the door and hovered in front of me. I whispered to my friend, "You aren't going to believe this, but I'm eye to eye with a hummingbird." The tiny jewel-toned busybody hung there, turning his head from side to side, as if checking out my trailer. Seeming pleased with the home I had made for myself, he flew off. I felt sort of proud, suddenly. I was safe and secure, and my life was my own again. "I'm going to make it," I told my friend on the phone. "I deserve to be happy again."

As summer passed, my dad and I got to recognize many of the hummingbirds individually. When I needed a lift, I had only to glance out my window at the feeders swaying in the breeze and the tiny, feathered bodies darting about on invisible wings. There were just enough of them shimmering outside in the sunlight. Just enough to make all the difference.

God does not lead His children around hardship,
but leads them straight through hardship....
And amidst the hardship,
He is nearer to them than ever before.
—OTTO DIBELIUS

SUMMER WILL COME AGAIN

STEPHANIE P. MARSHALL

Hannah was born October 14, 1996, weighing six pounds two ounces. After two days in the hospital, she came home to the nursery that my husband, Pierce, and I had prepared for her at our house in Dallas. Hannah was a good sleeper right from the start and took to nursing easily. But she didn't move around and kick like I'd seen other newborns do. At her two-week checkup, our pediatrician expressed concern about her muscle development. Then, a week later, Hannah was diagnosed with spinal muscular atrophy, an incurable genetic neuromuscular disease.

Pierce and I devoted ourselves to caring for her. We exercised her arms and legs and took her on long walks to stimulate her senses. "What did we do before we had Hannah?" Pierce asked me one morning as she lay in bed between us. "I can't remember," I said, stroking her downy skin. We laughed as Hannah cooed and reached out to grab my finger.

We were encouraged when she still appeared healthy at three months. But as the neurologist expected, by the time she was five months she couldn't swallow or breathe on her own. She went on an oxygen machine, and we had to tube-feed her.

Even smiling took more strength than she had to spare. Hannah slept most of the time, with Pierce and me gazing down at her in bed, ready to comfort her if she seemed restless. The hospice nurses prepared us: Hannah was dying.

One night when she was seven months old, our daughter had an unusually difficult time breathing, waking every hour distressed. We were relieved when she finally fell into a calm sleep. "She looks so peaceful," I whispered. Pierce smoothed Hannah's dark hair, and joy fluttered within me to see her looking so beautiful, even if it was for the last time. Hannah died the next morning.

At the funeral I was amazingly composed, glad to talk to everyone who came. But when had I ever had trouble talking about our precious baby girl? Even now I found joy in telling stories about her.

Back at home Pierce and I stood in the empty foyer. There was nothing more to do. No more feedings, no medicines, no arrangements to be made. There was only silence, and time. Pierce put his arms around me. "Let's go for a drive," he said.

Somehow we wound up at a movie. We walked in and sat way in the back. I stared at the screen, the action passing before me like so many random colors and sounds. *I haven't been to the movies since Hannah was born,* I thought.

The sun was setting as we got into the car. When Pierce turned onto Greenville Avenue, I knew we were headed for Restland Cemetery, where Hannah was buried.

American flags dotted the graves and hung from the fence that bordered the cemetery. *That's right,* I remembered, *it's Memorial Day weekend.* In the past, that holiday had meant barbecues, swimming and laughing with friends and family in the hot sun. It meant summer was finally here. But how could I think about summer when it was still winter in my heart? *I'll never know joy again,* I thought. I sat down beside Hannah's grave and started to cry. Pierce knelt next to me.

"Lucy, come back!" someone called. I lifted my head just in time to see what looked like an orange rocket coming at me. It was a dog! A short-haired, orange dog, legs too short for her body, with pointed ears that stood straight up.

She launched herself at me and licked my face, wagging her tail so her whole body wiggled. Two young, blond-haired boys stood near the fence calling, "Lucy! Lucy!" But she just danced around me, licking tears from my face and tripping over her feet. When I reached out to pet her, she kissed me smack on the lips. "Yuck!" I exclaimed and wiped my mouth on my shirtsleeve. I tried to hold the excited dog at arm's length. Pierce tried to intervene, but she squirmed right out of his hands and got me square on the kisser again. I felt something inside me loosen, and I started to laugh. "Lucy, leave those people alone!" the boys called. Lucy rolled over for a tummy scratch. Pierce obliged. Her tail waved back and forth, flattening the grass.

"She's not bothering us," I called back. Lucy licked me on the nose and then dashed back to the boys, who joined their family at another grave. A baseball pennant flapped on the fence near them, and I watched Lucy try to catch it. On the way home I shook my head over that spunky little dog. *Well, she made me laugh,* I thought. *I'll give her that.*

The respite from my grief didn't last. Without Hannah, I opened my eyes in the mornings aching for some reason to get up. Everyday errands seemed pointless. I moved through the hours on automatic pilot, numb and without any enthusiasm.

One day I was going over a list of recommended books on grief, and one in particular caught my eye. It was written by a counselor I'd met through the hospice chaplain. Reading her book, I could see she truly understood what I was going through. Still, Hannah had been dead only six weeks, and I couldn't bear to think of the lifetime without her that lay ahead.

"Maybe I need to join a support group," I said to Pierce one night. He encouraged me to give it a try. "For me, talking to you is enough, Stephanie. But maybe you need something more," he said.

I had high hopes when I arrived at my first meeting. The group leader talked about common stages of grief so that we would know what to expect and offered suggestions for getting through each one. I returned for the next session. Gradually I got to know the other parents and hear about the children they had lost.

One night in October, I hesitated before walking into the meeting. I was learning how to survive without Hannah, but maybe I'd gotten all the help I possibly could from the support group. Maybe there was no place I could go to get all the help I needed. *God, only you know the joy and laughter I lost when Hannah died. Help me find those moments of joy again.* I got out of the car to go to one last meeting.

As I settled into my usual chair, I tried to remember the last time I'd had a good laugh. The door behind me opened and a couple came in. I had spoken to them occasionally. Their name was Muir, and they didn't live far from Pierce and me. Tonight they brought one of their sons along, a blond-haired boy in a scout uniform. *That blond hair,* I thought. It made me recall a couple of blond-haired boys I'd seen not all that long ago. That day in the cemetery—I had laughed when those boys couldn't control their crazy little dog, Lucy.

All through the meeting I kept looking over at the boy, remembering the feeling of Lucy's cold nose poking my cheek when she bounced up to give me a kiss and the sight of her pudgy tummy as Pierce scratched her. I almost laughed all over again.

I approached the Muirs when the meeting was over. They introduced me to their son, whose name was Jess, and we began talking about our children. I told them Hannah was buried at Restland, back in Dallas.

"Matthew is buried there too," Bonnie Muir said. "Near the fence."

"By the baseball pennant?" I asked, remembering Lucy racing around below it.

"That's our flag," her husband replied. "The boys put it up."

The boys? I looked again at Jess. "Were you there on Memorial Day with your sons and your dog?" I asked. "A hyper orange dog?"

"That's Lucy!" Bonnie exclaimed. "And those poor people she ambushed—was that you and your husband? I'm sorry. I hope Lucy didn't disturb you."

"Disturb me?" I said. "She was just what I needed." And now, once again, when I was sure I would never know joy again, God had used that little dog to remind me that I could. And what more was there to live for every day than those moments of God-given joy?

And he that sat upon the throne said,
Behold, I make all things new.
—REVELATION 21:5

A GARDEN OF HOPE

JEANNE WHITE

When Ryan [White] was ill, I had no time for gardening. Now every single day I work in my yard. I plant tomatoes, blackberries, strawberries, roses, and lilies, and a few kinds of annuals and perennials. Early in the morning, just at that hour when I used to get up and fill the sink and get my son's medicines ready, I go out there and start up the day in my garden. I flip the Japanese beetles off the roses into a jar of water and cooking oil. I feed the two pretty fish in my pond, and trim off all the browning leaves and flower heads. We have three raccoons who empty my bird feeders every night, so in the morning I fill up the feeders again, and when that's done I give myself a laugh by singing out "Ring-a-ding-ding!" so the birds know their breakfast is ready. I mix a cup of water and a fourth of a cup of sugar and fill up the hummingbird feeders. Soon they're out whirring around me, as beautiful as the flowers whose nectar they love.

The dawn is like my state of mind these days. I look forward to everything. I love being married. Roy has made my life fun again. I look forward to every minute with him, to a long future, to growing old. Andrea has grown into a strong, smart, beautiful person. I look forward to everything her life has in store for us—adventures, travels, grandchildren. On the edge of the sky just beyond a cloud, I think I really see the end of the plague of AIDS. Every day, people whose lives once seemed to be finished are bursting with new health. The cure is coming. It's almost here. I feel like I will live to see it.

What greater gift can anyone receive than this sense of happy anticipation?

The garden has been my therapy. It's my other season besides Christmas. Here among the flowers and the bright fruit, when the light is brand new and everything is fresh and wet and the leaves are beaded up with dewdrops, I work in the household of nature and refresh my spirit.

In that lovely garden, I know exactly what my dad felt out on the lake under the shooting stars. I am sure, just as he was, that "there's got to be a better Being someplace behind all this." It seems to me that every weed I pull is a bit of grief I am learning to set aside, a tear I've weeded out so that good cheer can grow again.

I see in the faces of the flowers all the friends I have lost; I see my son's face. They are beautiful in the new morning, opening like smiles, and shining with hope.

Thank you, Lord, for another day.

Giving *and* Receiving Comfort

*It seems sometimes as if one were powerless to do
any more from within to overcome troubles,
and that help must come from without.*
—ARTHUR CHRISTOPHER BENSON

SUMMER OF SAM

MICHAEL J. FOX

New York—1994

SAM: Why do you keep wiggling your hand like that?

ME: I'm not really wiggling it, it just wiggles all by itself.

SAM: Is something wrong with it?

ME: Yeah . . . well no, not my hand. You know how every time you want to run or jump or throw a rock you have to tell your brain first, and then your brain tells your body what to do?

SAM: Your brain won't tell your hand to quit wiggling around?

ME: Exactly . . . the part of my brain that talks to my hand doesn't work too great.

SAM: You don't always wiggle.

ME: No, if I take a pill, it can fix the broken part of my brain for a while. But sometimes all I have to do is play a trick on it to make it stop.

SAM: You can trick your own brain?

ME: My own brain and my own hand—both at the same time. It's kind of a secret, but if I show you how, will you help me do it sometimes?

SAM: Yeah!

*P*arkinsonian Tremor is often referred to as a "resting tremor." That is, it occurs when the affected limb is at rest, or in an attitude of repose. (Interestingly, this doesn't apply to sleep, when, in all but the lightest phases, decreased brain activity virtually eliminates any muscle contraction and the tremor disappears.) Any willed movement can diminish or even suppress the tremor, at least momentarily, though it will reassert itself as soon as the limb settles into a new position. This is why, especially in the earliest stages, I was able to mask trembling through the most basic of manipulations: by picking up and putting down a coffee cup, twiddling a pencil or threading a coin through the fingers of my left hand. To keep this up at work or in public—another tiny repositioning every four or five seconds for hours at end—was an effective bit of sleight of hand, but it also exhausted me. And it was lonely work; whatever anybody thought I was doing at any given moment, I was at the same time also busy doing something else. I was, literally, driven to distraction.

In the spring of 1994, as I became more willing to recognize and accept P.D. as a fact of (my) life, I realized that I had been playing these tricks on my family as well. My unwillingness to let Tracy and Sam see a version of me any less than ideal put a certain distance between us that, I decided, would no longer do. So I lowered my guard at home, allowed myself to be open with my symptoms around my family. What a relief it was to relax for a change. Their reactions were a welcome surprise. Tracy, of course, didn't see anything she wasn't already acutely aware of. She was simply relieved and encouraged by my renewed trust. For Sam, now, the revelation of my symptoms was not the source of concern that I'd feared it would be; it was more a point of interest and curiosity of the kind that sparked the conversation at the top of this section. The utterly straightforward thrust of his questions taught me much about my son, and the way I found to share my reality with him taught me a lot about myself.

This is how it happened that when Sam was not quite five years old I taught him that if he saw my hand wiggling he could squeeze my thumb, or twist it slightly to make it stop.

"Then," I instructed, "count to five and give it another squeeze or twist, and you can trick it into staying still."

He experimented for a few minutes, at first counting aloud, and then in his head, making eye-contact and nodding to let me know it was time to give a squeeze. I could see his delight in getting the timing down, short-circuiting the wiggle every time. But once he understood that it *always* came back, I detected a slight look of *uh-oh, what have I gotten myself into*? "You know, Sam," I assured him, "this doesn't mean you have to do it every time. Not like it's your job or anything, only when you feel like it." His face brightened again.

"You can do it yourself still, right?"

"Right," I said.

Sam thought this over and then, "But I do it better."

"Definitely." I laughed. "And besides, I just like it when you hold my hand."

Sam's childlike willingness to accept my condition without dwelling on all its implications had a powerful influence on me. I'd conditioned myself to relate to the symptoms of the disease strictly as evidence of loss, of facility and freedom being taken away, but Sam's reaction suggested other possibilities. His curiosity awakened my own. If my condition could provide an opportunity to communicate so honestly and intimately with my son, what else might it bring? Clearly, to Sam, I was still "Dad," just "Dad with a wiggly hand." Was it possible that I could look at things the same way, that I was still me, just me plus Parkinson's?

Often that spring, I felt like a younger version of myself—like the Chilliwack me, pedaling my bike across the back lawn while dangling a garter snake, consumed once more with the possibilities of today. Yesterday's losses and tomorrow's trials were no longer the only poles of my existence—there was another place I could settle, and Sam had a lot to do with showing me where that was. The threat of time passing, hurrying me toward an uncertain fate, began to fade.

We grow by love . . . others are our nutriment.
—WILLIAM ELLERY CHANNING

LOVE DEEPER THAN GRIEF

GAIL ZIMMERMAN

It happened in the blink of an eye on a clear winter day. While mailing a letter, my mom was hit by a truck on the county road in front of my house. My husband, Jay, had shaken me awake and led me to where she was lying, pale and still in the flat light of morning. Staring at the brown pickup that had struck her, trembling as the paramedics loaded her into an ambulance, collapsing into Jay's arms when the doctor told me there was nothing he could do—I had everything jumbled in my mind, confused and distraught as one of my children after a nightmare. Except my nightmare was real.

Later that terrible afternoon I met with a sheriff's deputy. "Your mother was hit by Chris Youngen, a seventeen-year-old high school senior on her way to school," he told me. I'd seen Chris around our small town.

"As Miss Youngen rounded the corner right before your house, she was blinded by the sun's glare. She never saw your mother. No traffic laws were violated, so there won't be any charges filed."

Outrage rammed through my grief. "You mean some careless young driver kills my mother and gets off scot-free? You're not going to do anything?"

"I'm very sorry. We'll consider any new information that comes in. . . . You can sue her if you want."

"Will that bring back my mom?" I snapped.

Jay and I set about making funeral arrangements. When the kids came home from a neighbor's house that evening, I put on a brave face. But as four-year-old Tyler pushed *Mickey and the Beanstalk* into the VCR, I thought back to the night before, when Mom had watched the same video with Tyler, cuddling him in her lap.

I had just finished putting away the Tupperware fourteen-month-old Shannon had pulled out of a cabinet. Sitting down beside Mom on the couch, I had put my hand on my belly and asked, "Mom, do you really think I'll be able to manage with another one?" I was due in a month.

"Oh, Gail, there are worse things to handle than a baby," she'd said, laughing, and then wrapped her arm around me. "You'll do fine." How grateful I'd felt for her support, how cozy and safe with her staying over that night.

I wondered now if I would ever know that kind of peace and security again. My anxiety over the baby seemed trivial after what had happened. *You were right, Mom, there are worse things. Much worse.*

"Mommy, can Grandma come over and watch Mickey with me?" Tyler asked, pulling me away from my thoughts.

I motioned for him to come sit beside me. "Tyler, I have to tell you something." I smoothed back his hair as Mom used to. "You know how Daddy and I went to the hospital today? We went because Grandma died."

He gazed up at me, his blue eyes huge in his serious little face. "Will I get to see her again?"

"One day a long time from now we'll all be together," I said, blinking back tears.

"Are you sad, Mommy?"

"Yes, Mommy is very sad, honey. And it's okay to be sad. It's okay to cry if we feel like it."

"I think I might want to cry," he said. I stroked his soft cheek. Only Mom could have eased the dull ache in my chest. *Where do I find comfort?* I thought. Could anyone help me through this pain?

Several days later, at the visiting hours before Mom's funeral, a young, well-dressed woman approached me. It was Chris Youngen. Her face was ashen, her eyes red. "I don't know what to say, except that I am so sorry," she said, her voice barely a whisper.

"There is nothing to say," I responded. "Mom was a wonderful person and the world will never be the same." As I watched Chris walk away, anger flared inside me. That girl could go about her life as if nothing had happened. She could go to college, get married, have children. But my mom was gone forever. *How quick, how easy to destroy someone's life,* I thought. Just the blink of an eye and the light goes out. And words on an accident report weren't enough to explain it away and make it bearable. Chris's puffy cheeks and bloodshot eyes weren't enough. "Sorry" wasn't enough.

Somehow I forced myself through each day, though the thought of another baby was now overwhelming. Grief and bitterness demanded so much of my time. I couldn't wait till everyone else was in bed, so I could sit on the couch alone and cry the tears I choked back all day.

One afternoon I stood warming a bottle for Shannon. A snapshot of Mom was tacked to the kitchen cupboard in front of me. Every day since the accident Shannon had looked at that picture, asking, "Grandma?"

But that day she sat on the counter silently. I pointed to the picture and asked, "Who's this?" She looked up at me, wide-eyed, reaching for the bottle. Again I asked, "Who's in the picture, Shannon?"

She looked at the photo, then at me, sucking her fingers. The blank look in her eyes left me numb. Shannon had forgotten her grandma already. And the baby I was carrying would never know her.

Evan was born one month after the accident. I kept myself busy with the children and rarely went out. But even staying at home I couldn't avoid Chris. I often saw her truck pass by on her way to and from school. Every time its dusty brown hood came into view, I pictured the accident. *How convenient to dress up and go to a funeral and then just move on,* I thought.

I felt I was slipping into a deep, dark well. And even though my anger bore me down, I couldn't let go of it. Every prayer I tried to make disintegrated into unanswered questions and festering resentments. *It's so unfair,* I screamed inside. *God, how could you let her do this to us? How can I ever get beyond this when I have to see her all the time?*

It was as if I had been split in two: one part of me was the mother who kept everything going and kept smiling, for her kids' sake; the other was the daughter who, having lost her mother's protection, isolated herself from the rest of the world. It was this part that dragged me deeper into my grief and bitterness, unable to reach out to anyone for help—even God.

One day about six months after the accident I pushed Tyler and Shannon on the swings at the local playground, squinting against the harsh sunlight. Back and forth they swung, reminding me of my grief—receding a bit only to come back all the stronger. A crowd was watching a softball game nearby. If Mom were here, we might have gone to watch as well, but now I didn't want any part of it. Looking over the crowd, my gaze was caught by someone who didn't fit in with the enthusiastic spectators either. I realized it was Chris. I turned away, but was drawn to study her again. *Maybe I should try to talk to her,* I thought. *Why bother?* I instantly told myself. *She's at a ball game: She doesn't care what happened.* But her expression made it clear her mind wasn't on the game.

A huge cheer from the crowd woke Evan. I tried to soothe his wailing. "It's all right, baby." I bent my head low over him, rocking him gently.

"Are these your children?" someone asked. I looked up. It was Chris.

I nodded.

"They're beautiful," she said. Then she asked hesitantly, "How are you doing?"

"The children keep me busy," I replied. A charged silence hung between us. "How have you been?" I finally asked.

"Oh, you shouldn't ask about me after all I've put you through," she said.

How often I had imagined confronting her, demanding, "Do you know how miserable you've made us?" Yet now that we were face to face, I felt a rush of compassion. "Not a day goes by that I don't think of you, Chris."

"Me too," she said. "Every day when I go by your house, I slow down and look in. I have wanted so badly to stop and see you, but I was afraid."

So she hasn't put us behind her.

"To know I'm responsible for someone's death . . . I can't describe it. I can't believe you'll even speak to me. You have every right in the world to tell me to go away and leave you alone forever."

"It can't be easy for you either," I managed to say. Her face stiffened and I thought she was going to cry. It had been easier to think of her as careless and unfeeling, but now, for the first time, I put myself in her place. What would it be like to cause a death, to be reminded of it by the whispers of your community, to pass by the victim's family every day? "Chris, would you like to come over sometime so we could talk?"

She gave me a hopeful look. "I would like that very much. Thank you."

As I waited for her to arrive for lunch later that week, I did not think about what I would say to her or how I might feel. I only knew I had reached the bottom of my grief, and she was the one person who could help me up again. *Dear God,* I prayed, *only you know how hard I've struggled with this. Please be with me.*

When Chris came, we had lunch with the kids, eating little as we made small talk. Then I tucked in the kids for a nap and we sat down with an album filled with pictures of Mom. "Can you tell me about her?" Chris said.

"You would have liked Mom," I said. "She was so kind, so giving. Everyone loved her."

We flipped through the album. There were so many things I needed to ask Chris, so many things only she knew about my mother's last moments. Finally, I took a deep breath. "How did it happen?" I started.

"I'd scraped the windows that morning, but they fogged up again," she said. "As I turned the corner I saw nothing but blinding white. I tried to pull over. Then I heard a thud. At first I thought I'd hit an animal. But then I saw your mother and I ran to get help. I keep thinking, 'Why didn't I stop sooner?' It just happened so fast."

The words came easier after that, and we talked for a long while. By the time I showed her to the door, we were both spent. Suddenly she turned to face me again. "How can you do this?" she whispered, shaking her head. "Invite me into your house and talk with me all afternoon after what I've done?"

"Chris, it is only by the grace of God," I murmured, hugging her tightly.

Our words didn't make everything all right, but they were the first precious steps out of the darkness. Her apology was all she could give me, just as forgiveness was all I could give her. Yet somehow that was enough to make a start. And, slowly, out of so much pain, grew a deep and lasting friendship. Today Chris visits often with her son, born on the seventh anniversary of Mom's death.

I will always miss Mom, but I know she would have wanted me to move on. For me, the only way out of grief was to reach out to the woman responsible for my mother's death, and to allow God's love to heal us both.

Blessed be God . . . who comforteth us in all our tribulation,
that we may be able to comfort them which are in any trouble.
—2 CORINTHIANS 1:3–4

MICHAEL'S GIFT

M. FRAN RYBARIK

he year 1993 was one of graduations for our family. Our youngest son completed high school, our oldest son turned twenty-one, and I completed a master's degree in public health. My husband and I were gearing up for the "empty nest," with both boys off to college. It seemed like a good time for me to graduate to a new job, which would utilize my new health education skills in addition to my nursing background.

The next Sunday, I spotted a newspaper advertisement from a local hospital for the RTS national program director. I wasn't quite sure what that meant, so I called to find out more. I learned that the hospital had developed bereavement training for healthcare professionals, based on their clinical experiences in meeting the needs of patients who had lost a baby during pregnancy or shortly after birth. Initially named Resolve Through Sharing, they now called it RTS. It sounded interesting.

I was honored to be offered the position, but knew there would be a steep learning curve. Bereavement care was not part of my basic nursing education—and, I discovered, was a gap for many other professionals in healthcare. Not only would I work with other healthcare professionals across the country, but also I could learn more about a new topic—grief and loss—and improve the care of women and their families. This job was a health educator's dream come true. What I didn't recognize at the time was that my personal experiences would play a significant role, too.

The first few months were spent reading and learning about perinatal bereavement. It was helpful for my "head" to learn the facts and the history, but my heart led me to the stories of the bereaved parents whose pregnancies had ended early, whose babies had been born still, or whose babies had died shortly after birth. Their unique stories were told with the same heartfelt care—whether it had been two days or twenty years since they lost their baby. These parents weren't wallowing in grief and misery. They had learned that grief is about remembering. They didn't want to forget their babies—no matter how short their time together may have been or how long ago it might have been. When people tell their stories, they are capable of healing themselves.

And so, a few months into this new job, I found myself reflecting on my personal experience with loss—a miscarriage at ten or twelve weeks gestation, twenty years earlier.

It all began right after Christmas in 1973. We were living in a small town in Illinois when I found out I was pregnant. I remember being very surprised and upset by this news—another baby was not in the plan right then. My husband, David, traveled a lot for work and our baby, Scott, was only five months old.

Then things became very complicated. David left for an East Coast job assignment on New Year's Day. He came back early—with a possible diagnosis of cancer in the form of Hodgkin's disease. In the meantime, my doctor suspected something was wrong with the pregnancy—the egg may have implanted in the tube (ectopic) instead of in the uterus.

The rest of January was a blur. We traveled to Chicago to see specialists—blood tests for David and ultrasounds for me. We learned that David did not have cancer, but the good news was short-lived.

The ultrasound results couldn't rule out an ectopic pregnancy. Because my health and future ability to bear a child could be endangered, the doctor recommended exploratory surgery. Unforeseen complications caused the simple procedure to become major abdominal surgery. The outcome was another surprise—the baby was right where it should be.

We were beginning to believe that this pregnancy was meant to be, after all. Then, in the middle of a cold February night, the pregnancy ended in a miscarriage. We made another trip to the hospital, this time with a very small, perfectly formed baby in a plastic container. We named him Michael.

During my overnight hospital stay, I couldn't sleep, so the night nurse stayed in my room. She was very kind, and I felt very well cared for—at least physically. Although we talked about a lot of things, we never talked about the pregnancy, its outcome, or what to expect when I went home.

By the end of February, our lives had changed dramatically. I was going through a revolving range of emotions—guilt for not wanting to be pregnant; relief that the pregnancy had ended (because we were sure that something would be very wrong with this baby after all he'd been exposed to in those few short weeks); and depression. My feelings about the unexpected, unplanned, unwanted pregnancy had shifted over the weeks; I found myself grieving for this little baby who seemed to try so very hard to be born. It was difficult for me to find the energy to care for our son, Scott, and we invested little time in our marriage. We never even celebrated the good news that David didn't have cancer. Fortunately, my parents and our neighbors spent a lot of time with Scott and filled in the gaps for us—especially by providing hugs, tears, and sympathetic shoulders.

That summer we moved to Michigan, and our lives moved on, too. Another son, Brian, was born in 1975.

But it wasn't until my new job came along that we finally took time to review the devastating winter of 1974. Early in 1995, after more than twenty years had passed since Michael's death, David and I finally had a long talk about Michael. So many questions were asked. What would our lives be like now if he had been born? Would I have pursued the career opportunity in bereavement? We realized the importance of remembering Michael as a part of our family. We talked with our children about the experience of miscarriage and about their brother. We inscribed Michael's name on a memorial for unborn babies.

People often ask me about my work in bereavement. How can you do such depressing work? You know what, though? It isn't depressing! Because I know my work makes a difference to those who experience this type of loss, it is a source of great comfort to me personally. Michael left me the gift of understanding bereaved parents and allowing me to help them heal. I am utterly grateful for the legacy of his brief life: helping me help others.

We not only need to be willing to give,
but also to be open to receiving from others.
—ON HOPE

A SIMPLE CURE

MARION BOND WEST

I was at the end of my rope in 1970. My twin boys were in their "terrible twos," and I simply couldn't control them. Just trying to keep them still was a struggle. I never knew where they'd go next. The living room was a minefield of toys. The carpet wore the scars of countless spills. The morning alarm was a call to battle, and by each evening I knew I'd lost again.

It had been much easier with my girls, who were eight and ten. They were so quiet and well-behaved I'd been able to get plenty of time for myself—reading, doing volunteer work, even taking art lessons.

"It's so convenient for you," I griped to my husband, Jerry. "You can go to work and get away. But I have to deal with this mess day in and day out." Jerry tried to assure me that the house didn't have to look perfect. Well, there was no chance of that, what with the unwashed dishes and laundry piling up day by day. Some days I didn't even get out of my bathrobe. What was the point?

I felt like a failure. It seemed like nothing could make me feel hopeful again. I was so far gone even prayer brought me little comfort.

My friends urged me to seek help. I finally became so sick and tired of feeling sick and tired that I gave in. The counselor I went to see had four children just like I did, only hers were all grown. Obviously she had managed to raise them just fine.

She had so much energy and enthusiasm that it wore me out just to look at her.

When I finished spilling out my problems, the counselor asked, "Mrs. West, have you ever heard of Dr. Karl Menninger? He always said there was one surefire way for people who were depressed to feel better. They should find someone who needs help and help them. Will you try it?"

I shook my head vaguely. I could barely drag myself out of bed in the morning. How could I possibly help anyone else?

"You mentioned you used to do hospital volunteer work, Mrs. West. Why don't you find a day-care center to put your boys in a couple half-days a week and go back to volunteering?"

I was way too weary to argue with her so I agreed to try it. As it turned out Jerry and the girls thought it was a good idea too, and the twins were only too thrilled to have an exciting new place to go twice a week.

The following week I went to Athens General Hospital and joined six other new volunteers in watching a demonstration on how to make a bed properly. *I didn't leave a house of unmade beds to make up hospital beds,* I thought. *Besides, right now I feel better suited to lying in one than making up one.*

So I went to the office of the hospital's new recreational therapist and volunteered for her program instead.

"Okay, I'll give you a list of patients," she said. "Just take these paints and brushes, knock on their doors, and ask them if they want to paint. Remember to smile big and act positive!"

I hoped those art lessons I'd taken would come in handy. I took the list and painting supplies and rode the elevator up to the hospital's second floor. I stopped into the ladies' room and stood before mirror. I looked so serious I scared myself. Mustering up a pale imitation of a smile, I turned and headed for the first patient's room.

"Hi, I'm Marion," I said. "Would you like to paint?"

"No," came the answer. "And please make sure you close the door when you leave." It happened again and again. No one wanted to paint and I felt stupid asking. But I kept at it, mainly so I could say that I'd given it my best shot. I finally came to the last person on my list. While I knocked on that door, I glanced at the patient's information: NAME: Coy Pritchett. AGE: Twenty. CONDITION: Kidney complications/quadriplegic/depression.

I froze for a moment. This man was totally paralyzed. What could I do for him? I cautiously opened the door and stepped inside. I was staring at the heels of a patient on a Stryker frame, a huge wheel-like contraption that keeps a patient immobile while turning him to prevent pressure sores. At the moment Coy was facedown. "Hi, I'm Marion. Would you like to paint a picture?" I asked automatically, before realizing how absurd that must sound to someone who couldn't move his arms.

"Shoot, yeah," he answered. Yes? For a moment I wanted to run from the room, turn in my name tag, and flee back to my wreck of a house. But Coy was waiting on me, so I went over to him. Putting down the painting supplies, I got down on my hands and knees and looked up into his face. He had a dark crew cut and a smile a mile wide. "Hi, Marion," he said. "I think I'd like to paint a rabbit—like the ones I was always seeing in the woods before I got like this. Do you think maybe you could put the brush in my mouth?"

Would it work? I broke a long-handled brush in two. "Here, I'll wrap some tape around it so it's smooth," I said. Carefully I eased the brush into Coy's mouth. I mixed up some colors and held up a canvas under his face. He began to paint. I kept the board as still as I could, though my back and arms ached from the awkward position. After a few minutes the rabbit began to take shape. *Not bad,* I thought. We took a break and I held up a cup of water for him to drink through a straw.

"Tell me about yourself, Marion. I don't get many visitors besides my folks," he said. "You got a family?"

I nodded.

"You must be a great mom," he said. "You're so patient." If he only knew. "I got me a son too," he continued. "His mama left with him when I got in the diving accident a year ago. I don't blame her, though." I looked at Coy carefully. I sensed it wasn't so much the prospect of painting that made him welcome me as a need for personal contact. *God, I know I might not have much to give right now, but please help me be a comfort to this young man.*

The next time I came to the hospital I went straight to Coy's room. We painted and when we needed a rest we talked. I got permission to visit just him during each of my four-hour sessions. Coy was hungry for any story of life outside the hospital's walls. We talked a lot about our families. Coy's parents lived nearby and often came to see him. He always painted animals or plants he'd seen in the woods near his house. Once I smuggled a baby blue jay into the hospital as a treat for him. I set it on his chest and he imitated its call. Other times he whistled or sang country songs during our breaks.

I began looking forward to my visits with Coy, checking on his progress, helping him express himself through painting. I found myself more patient with the twins too, knowing I'd get a break from them every few days. Painting with Coy in his hospital room, I felt like we were off in another world. I was so focused on him I didn't have time to think about my own problems. And when I was with him, I found I didn't feel so tired anymore.

"So what stunt did the boys pull this time?" he asked one day when I was fretting over the twins.

"Jeremy actually tried to climb up inside the chimney yesterday! He said he wanted to see how Santa Claus did it."

Coy's laughter rang off the room's walls. "Your kids are something else!" he said. Incredibly I started laughing too, for the first time in months. No doubt about it, my kids did keep things interesting. "Yes, but *what* else?" I asked and doubled over laughing again.

I started getting up earlier, even on days I wasn't visiting Coy. I'd clean up the kitchen before the twins woke up. Sometimes I'd walk the girls to the bus stop. The piles of grimy dishes and dirty clothes still looked daunting—but not unmanageable.

One day I walked into Coy's room to find him lying in bed with a sheet pulled over him. A nurse quickly explained, "Coy's having a bad day and doesn't want to be bothered." After she left I pulled the sheet off Coy's face.

"Coy, it's Marion. Come on, let's paint."

He wouldn't open his eyes.

"Coy, don't you want to finish that flower you were working on?"

Still no response. Finally I took some water and flicked it at him. A smile played around the corners of his mouth and he opened one eye, then the other. "Okay, okay, you win," he said with a laugh. "Let's paint."

He finished the flower picture that day. I took it and seven other paintings Coy had done to a frame shop and laid them out for the owner. Among them was an owl, a squirrel, an old oak tree. "He paints with his teeth," I said. "I can only afford to have one framed. Which one do you like the best?"

The owner studied the paintings for a moment, then said, "No charge. I want them all done right. They deserve it."

They were finished a couple of weeks later. At my next session with Coy I placed the eight beautifully framed pictures under his face.

"Man, oh man," he breathed. "These are really incredible. Thank that man for me, Marion."

A few days later, I headed back from the bus stop after seeing the girls off and picked up the newspaper on my way inside. I sat down at the kitchen table and glanced out the window at some robins chittering in the trees. *Wouldn't Coy just love to paint you little darlings!* I thought.

I turned to look at the paper and gasped. There on the front page was a picture of a smiling Coy and his framed paintings. Apparently, they were going to be hung in the hospital's lobby! I was so excited I decided I would wake the boys, so I could read the article aloud to them.

As I got up, I caught sight of the quote below Coy's picture. "Life sure is sweet," he said. *Yes, it is,* I thought. Certainly not perfect or easy but definitely sweet, especially when there are people like Coy to remind you of the joy in the world.

Nowadays there are more ways than ever to treat depression. For me, what it took to start feeling better was to reach out to someone who needed me. But not more than I needed him.

Find out how much God has given you and from it take what you need; the remainder is needed by others.

—St. Augustine

Two Are Better Than One

Luci Swindoll

Sometimes I think I'm the Lone Ranger. I'm the picture of solitude and independence. I entertain myself for days with no help from anyone.

But that isn't always the case. Every now and then I feel the need for connectedness. I want to be surrounded by my circle of friends. Being alone just doesn't cut it. That's what happened last summer when I started out thinking I was the Lone Ranger.

I was in Ireland with a friend. On the day we were scheduled to fly to Scotland, I awakened feeling ill, chilled and nauseated. My friend suggested we reschedule our flight, but I insisted I'd be fine. I fully intended to rise up and walk, to get myself packed, dressed, to the airport, and on to the next country on our itinerary. I was sure I wouldn't need any help, being the Lone Ranger and all. . . . In the meantime, I went back to bed.

When I awakened from my feverish stupor, my traveling companion had gathered up my things, packed my bags, and made all the arrangements for us to leave. She asked again if I wanted to delay our departure. Of course not! I insisted I'd be fine. The minute we climbed in the cab, I fell sound asleep.

Arriving at the airport, again I heard, "Do you want to leave later?" Of course not! I insisted I'd be fine. So while I rested in a wheelchair inside the terminal, she stood in line, checked in our bags, and collected our boarding passes. I fell fast asleep in the chair.

This went on all day, with my insisting I could make it on my own while she did both my part and hers. I fell asleep every time I found a place to sit.

Ultimately, we arrived at the hotel in Scotland. While she made sure our possessions were brought to the room, found a drugstore, and bought medicine, I crawled into bed.

It wasn't until the next day I figured out how I got there. I had had a caretaker in my time of need . . . one who joyfully provided for me when I was oblivious to her acts of kindness and hard work.

That's the way life is, isn't it? We need each other. Scripture says two are better than one. We're instructed to love, pray for, care about, accept, forgive, serve, encourage, and build up one another.

I love that about my partners in the Joyful Journey conferences. We bebop all over the country watching out for each other. We serve one another joyfully, from the heart. When one of us is down, we rally to her. When one celebrates, we rejoice together. We're a team. We never anticipated this kind of bonding, but bonded we are.

People need each other—no matter how much we insist we don't. Nobody is an island, an entity unto herself, or a Lone Ranger. We're in this thing called *community*, and part of the joy of community is sharing the weight. The weight of burdens, losses, loneliness, and fear.

Look around you, my friend. Who's there for you? And who are you there for? Take a careful look. Even those who insist they can make it on their own may just be waiting for you to reach out and help. Be there and available. Even the Lone Ranger had a sidekick.

When you dig another out of their troubles,
you find a place to bury your own.
—AUTHOR UNKNOWN

MY PERFECT NEIGHBOR

PATRICIA BUTLER DYSON

Hi, I'm Jerri," she said. "Jerri with an i." My neighbor stood at my front door with her two little boys. Ten years younger and at least ten pounds thinner than me, she had silky blonde hair and a healthy tan.

"Come on in," I said. I'd arranged this meeting so my five-year-old son, Brent, could get to know some other boys from the neighborhood who were starting kindergarten in the fall. He would be a little more confident on that first day of school if he just had one friend. I'd gotten the class list from school and noticed that Marty Bradford lived a few blocks from us.

"This is Marty," Jerri said. Her son marched up to Brent and stood face-to-face with him in the hall, sizing him up.

"Brent, why don't you take Marty to the backyard and show him your tree house?" I suggested.

"Go ahead," his mother urged. The two boys scrambled off.

"Y'all come sit down for a minute," I said.

Jerri gestured to the child clinging to her leg. "Max is shy."

She followed me into the living room and sat on the sofa, Max perched in her lap. Jerri was everything I wished I could be: elegant, composed, sunny-tempered.

She talked about the exercise class she and Max took together and the bread she baked from scratch—yeast, dough, and all. There wasn't even a hint of conceit in her voice, yet she stirred up in me a vague feeling of inadequacy. But nothing pained me as much as watching her with that sweet-faced, brown-eyed boy in her lap.

"How old is he?" I finally asked.

"Max?" she said. "Four. He and Marty are eighteen months apart."

Brent's younger brother would have been four too. I almost said it out loud, told Jerri what we had been through in the past months since Blake died, but I stopped myself. I couldn't confide in a stranger, especially one whose life seemed so together.

"I'd better run," Jerri said. "I'm baking my bread for the week."

"I'll bring Marty home in an hour," I responded.

"Super." Then she and her younger son were off.

From that point on, Brent had regular play dates with Marty. They built forts in our backyard and held imaginary sword fights in Brent's room. I was grateful my son had a new friend, but seeing Jerri always made me feel worse about myself. She was so cool and confident. She had moved here from up North when her husband transferred, but even our hot, humid East Texas weather hardly had an effect on her.

I convinced myself that once kindergarten started I wouldn't have to see her so often. But the day before school began she called and announced, "Marty wants to ride his bike to school tomorrow with Brent. How about us all going together?"

"Okay," I said hesitantly. "I haven't biked in a while. . . ."

"It'll be fun!" she interrupted. "We'll meet you at the corner of Westgate and Elaine at 7:45 sharp."

The next morning after breakfast, I unearthed my bike from a corner of the garage and Brent hopped on his.

Marty and Jerri were waiting at the corner, Max in a baby seat on the back of his mother's bike. "Hi, guys!" Jerri said. "Ready for the big day?"

"Yeah!" Brent said, smiling. "I guess so," I said. Then—on a day that should have only been about the future and the wonders it would hold for our two boys—Jerri sent me plunging into the past, into my sorrow.

She was staring at the empty baby seat on the back of my bike. "Do you have a little one I haven't met yet?" she asked.

"I did," I said, trying hard to keep my voice steady. *The same age as your Max. The same blond hair, the same brown eyes, the same smile beneath a bike helmet.* "Brent's brother, Blake, was three when he died of meningitis last year. I just haven't been up to removing the seat yet."

"Oh, Pat, how awful for you," Jerri said. "I'm so sorry."

"Thanks," I said quickly. "Hey, Marty, what a neat bike!" I didn't want to talk about my grief.

For the next few weeks, as summer mellowed into autumn, Jerri and I would meet and ride with our boys to and from school. Little by little I learned more about her. She said her husband was often away on business and that as welcoming as people were in Texas, she hadn't made many friends. No matter what she said, her life still sounded perfect, whether she was sewing Halloween costumes for her kids or baking cookies or cakes for the church bazaar or rushing back from an aerobics class. The hardest thing for me each morning was seeing young Max in the seat behind her, dressed in his Peanuts pajamas. But I choked back my feelings.

One morning it pained me so much I came back home and threw down my bike helmet in a rage. "Dear God," I cried out, "why is everything in her life so perfect when parts of mine are so empty?"

Later that afternoon our little caravan was making its way home when suddenly

Marty let out a howl as we turned the corner at Westgate. "Mommy!" he cried. "I forgot the popcorn we made at school. Can we go back and get it?"

"Absolutely not," Jerri said, with surprising sharpness. "Marty, you must learn to keep track of your things."

Brent gave me a woeful look, and I knew he felt bad for his friend. So when we parted ways with the Bradfords, I gave Brent a wink and we headed back to the school. Marty's bag of popcorn was just where he left it, in his cubby in their classroom. Pedaling as fast as we could, we rode to Marty's house. Brent ran up and rang the doorbell and I stood behind him. Jerri opened the door, revealing a trail of toys and clothes littering her foyer.

"We got Marty's popcorn," I said.

Jerri frowned. She held a broken toy in her hand. "I wish you hadn't, Pat," she said. "Marty's so irresponsible. I'm trying to teach him a lesson."

A dozen angry retorts sprang to my lips. Instead of the thank-you I deserved, I was being reprimanded. "I'm sorry," I said coldly. "I had no idea."

The next morning I led Brent on a different route to school so that we would be sure to avoid the Bradfords. "What about Marty and his mommy?" Brent asked plaintively.

"They'll catch up with us," I said.

At school I gave Brent a quick kiss good-bye, then biked home. I sailed into the garage and was starting to yank down the door when Jerri careened into my driveway on her bike with Max strapped in his seat.

"Pat, wait!" Jerri hollered. "I have to talk to you."

I stood beside my bike, staring down.

"Where were you this morning?" she asked. "We missed you."

"We left early," I replied.

"Pat, please forgive me," Jerri said. "I've hurt your feelings and I'm sorry. I've just been so stressed out lately." I was surprised to hear a quaver in Jerri's voice.

"Forget it." I turned to go inside.

"You wouldn't understand," Jerri said. "You have everything under control. You're such a good mother, you keep a neat house, and Brent is a happy, well-adjusted little boy. With my husband gone so much, I'm like a single parent. I feel like a failure next to you. You're so together."

"Me? Together?" I whirled back toward her. "Do you know how miserable I feel each morning after I leave you? Do you know how it crushes my heart to see Max every day, the same age as Blake and looking so much like him?"

"How would I?" Jerri said quietly. "You've never let me into your life."

Then it dawned on me: had Jerri also been keeping her feelings to herself, hiding her pain from anyone who might comfort her? She hadn't lost a child, but she was going through a tough time of her own. Maybe Jerri and I had been brought together to share our problems, not hide them.

"I'm just trying to be a good mother," Jerri went on, "to do the right things. The way you do, Pat. I wish I could be like you."

"But I don't sew costumes or bake bread. And lately I've been so depressed I can hardly make it from day to day." The tears started coming.

Jerri got off her bike, unbuckled Max, and set him down on the grass, then put her arms around me. "I had no idea what you were going through," she said.

"I was keeping a stiff upper lip."

"So was I."

"Maybe we're more alike than we know," I said as I wiped my face. Instead of reaching out, I had withdrawn, and in a way so had Jerri. We were both feeling inadequate and had been unable to say it. "We're not good at putting up fronts."

Jerri nodded. "I know now is not the time, but someday, Pat, would you tell me about Blake?" she asked softly.

"I'd like that. Thank you. And this afternoon . . ."

"Meet you at the corner of Westgate and Elaine at 2:45?"

"I'll be there." I scooped up Max, touched his soft cheek, and buckled him into his bike seat. "See you later, alligator." He blew me a kiss as he and Jerri rode off into the crisp, bright morning.

In the day when I cried thou answeredst me,
and strengthenedst me with strength in my soul.
—PSALM 138:3

COMPASSION WITHOUT COMPROMISE

RUBY STEED

uring the summer of 1993, right in the middle of graduate school, I was a volunteer at Mother Teresa's Home of the Destitute Dying in Calcutta. I never thought it would be easy, but when I awoke in the oppressive heat each morning I wondered how I would get through the day. First I had to wash the patients' saronglike garments (called *lungis*). Then I helped serve meals and clean up. I mopped the ward and helped patients with their personal hygiene. The work was unending. Soon I became sick. *This is horrible,* I thought. *I feel as weak as the patients I'm supposed to take care of.*

One morning after Mass, Sister JosMa came up to me. "Wait here," she said. "Mother will see you today. She likes to meet all of the volunteers herself." My pulse quickened. I couldn't believe she could find time for me.

Sitting on a balcony bench overlooking the clinic's walkways, I watched Mother Teresa as she hurried to her appointments. Finally, not wanting to intrude on her schedule, I got up to leave when suddenly she came over and asked how I was faring.

"I'm not handling India well, Mother," I confessed.

Reaching up with her strong hands, she pulled my head down to hers. "Yah. Yah. India can be very hard. But you must pray to Jesus for strength and you must come to Mass." There was compassion but no compromise in her voice. From her robe she pulled out a small metal crucifix, which she kissed. "You must put this on the chain around your neck," she said. She rested her hand on my chest for an instant, then left.

That cross remained around my neck through the rest of that long, hot summer in India, then through the rest of graduate school, a new career in social work, and a bout with cancer. When I say my prayers at night I can still hear Mother's heavily-accented English: "You must pray to Jesus for strength." Strength she shared with so many others.

Words *of* Comfort

He is a man of sense who does not grieve
for what he has not, but rejoices in what he has.
—EPICTETUS

BLESSINGS IN DISGUISE

FAITH BALDWIN

onight I was talking to a close friend about a situation in her family, and she said, "Maybe it's a blessing in disguise." That is an old saying. It is one that many people laugh at as a cliché. But it can be truth itself. Visualize a woman who has bought a house, having managed to save a little and move from a rented apartment. As are most houses, it was purchased with a mortgage lashed to it. This disturbs her. She hates the mortgage as if it were a deadly personal enemy. Yet, for the first time in her life, she is saving money; she has to, in order to meet the interest. She does so regularly; she has an equity in her house; she has a place in her community; she is, as the banks say, a good risk. That which she considers a millstone about her neck is really a blessing . . . in disguise.

There is a man who had, suddenly, an illness. His family after his return from the hospital put all their intelligence to bear on the things which would make him well; particularly they were aware of all that, to heal him, would have to be withheld. Later, when he had recovered, his work took him to a different state. He was well, he was fine, he was also on his own. His original trouble had been eradicated and did not return, so, although he had been warned to lose weight and had done so, he proceeded happily to regain it. He found himself presently in another hospital, not with the illness of the preceding year but with what was apparently an overstrained heart. Perhaps this, too, is a blessing in disguise, and from now on he will be careful.

Sometimes the blessings are so well disguised that we do not see beneath the mask until months, even years thereafter.

Are you a step-retracer? I am, and this peculiar quality is not exclusively a feminine trait. Physically, I retrace so many steps that, laid end to end, they would carry me, in a day's time, downtown and back. Turn me loose in a kitchen and I run between pots and pans, sink, range and refrigerator. I carry things endlessly, being too impatient to put them on the tray which would save the steps. I never go to bed and stay there. I am up and down. I have left one pair of glasses downstairs or forgotten to turn out the outside lights. I didn't bring up the book I'd laid aside to read in bed. I have mislaid the TV program. I was certain I had taken everything upstairs with me but, no, there are at least three things I am sure I can't live without during the night. And I always forget to take a handkerchief from pocket, purse or drawer.

It's a tiring thing, retracing steps.

I suppose one reason I do this is that I think of other things, and never see what is in front of me. I can leave a room six times and go back—often because of pure laziness. In order to turn on the lights which flood the enclosed stairway I have only to go into the entry hall and touch a switch. But to do that, I must cross the study and living room. So, I turn out the study lights and creep upstairs in the dark. I am always losing my way and crashing into doorways, mantelpieces and the like. Once in the upper hall, I turn the lights on, but by that time I am battered and bruised.

The other night I managed to take everything up with me: a fur coat, a hat, a handbag and a tall glass of orange juice. I saved myself steps by putting on the hat and the coat for the brief journey, but I didn't turn on the light. Just try going up thirteen steps in pitch-darkness with a glass of orange juice in one hand!

Introspection can be overdone. But sometimes it is wise to retrace the steps of your life, which have brought you to where you are now—to see why you took so many steps in the first place . . . why you went back again and again and why you didn't turn on the lights when all it would have cost you was a little effort.

Now, as I look at the clock, measuring the distance to the entry hall and the light switch, and look unhappily at what passes for typewritten pages, I am struck with the logical thought that, before I go upstairs, I must retrace my mental steps. I must go back to November and Thanksgiving which set me to writing and thinking of gratitude . . . thankfulness for spiritual joy, for faith, for the direct road, for the blessing in disguise. And even for the ability to laugh at myself when I consider all my unnecessary steps. No efficiency engineer would tolerate me and my lack of method.

So November goes quietly or stormily into the Christmas month, which I love, whatever it brings in weather, and there is another blessing; another December for giving and loving and rejoicing, and for knowing that Thanksgiving is for always.

Retracing the mental steps I know that much has been given me since last Thanksgiving, and some things, denied. And I think I've learned how a Thanksgiving prayer should be fashioned. I've said it before, but here it is again:

"Thank You, Father," I would say, "for all You have given me, are giving and will give; and also for all that has been withheld, for if You withhold, then I know it is best for me."

It takes quite a spell of living to learn to be thankful for the things you haven't had, even though you may have prayed for them, but your Father in Heaven knows your needs.

*Why art thou cast down, O my soul? . . . hope thou in God:
. . . who is the health of my countenance . . .*
—PSALM 42:11

BURIED SORROW

MARIANNE FARRIN

The woman pulled me aside after church. "I understand you're a therapist," she said, not quite looking me in the eye. I nodded and we walked over to a bench along Fifth Avenue and sat. "It's not like things are terrible in my life," she went on, almost apologetically. "It's just that I feel empty inside. Almost numb. I'll smile and laugh but not really feel anything. Most of the time I'm . . . faking it."

My training as a counselor told me what the nature of this woman's trouble might be. That's why I gave her my card and asked her to make an appointment. Yet what really made me grasp her predicament was not so much a professional knowledge but my own personal experience. You see, half my life I felt much the same way, weighed down by a burden I didn't understand. In fact I had so little to compare it to I often wondered if this was the way everyone felt.

On the outside my life was fine . . . a devoted, successful husband and five bright, healthy children. On the inside, though, I felt dead. I went through life faking happiness and trying to live up to the joy people thought I should feel. But the whole time I wondered what would happen if anyone found out how I really felt. It took me thirty painful years to admit to myself that something was wrong.

I was born in war-torn Germany, and among my earliest memories in Berlin was the nightly horror of Allied planes raining bombs from the sky. One night, we were huddled in the basement, waiting for the all-clear, when there was a tremendous explosion. Our apartment building had been hit. My father, who was very brave, led us to the safety of a friend's house, where I was put to bed and told to go to sleep.

"Poppi, Poppi, don't go," I remember pleading. I was only five years old. "Hush, be brave," he answered. "Don't cry. Just go to sleep." He turned off the light and left the room.

Now as an adult I can see the scene from my parents' point of view. They needed time to talk to the other adults, take stock, and make plans. But I was terrified, alone in that strange bedroom. *Be brave. Don't cry.*

We managed to escape to Denmark. My mother's family lived there. By that time, though, my father had been conscripted into the German army and shipped to the Russian front. Occasionally we got a letter. The last came in 1944. "Be a good student," he wrote me in a shaky hand. "Make your Poppi proud."

We had no more news for five years. Mother tried to find out about Poppi. I worked hard in school. Word finally came via the Red Cross that my father had died in a Russian prisoner-of-war camp near the end of the war. There was no funeral, no body. There was just us, and Mother didn't want to talk much about what had happened. I accepted the unspoken message: We had to get on with our lives and bury the past, with all its pain and sorrow. We emigrated to the United States. My tenth-grade year my mother and sister and I settled in Hollywood.

What a stark contrast to the somberness of postwar Europe! Hollywood High was like a movie set—everyone had golden tans and perfect teeth. I told myself if I smiled like them I'd fit in. I dated the captain of the football team and I became my class's vale-dictorian. With God's help, I hoped I could be as happy as everyone else seemed to be.

I went to Stanford on a full scholarship. There, too, I faced the world with a smile no matter what. I met my husband, Jim, a handsome athlete at the business school. He got a good job with an international corporation. Our first assignment was in Australia. We settled in a nice house in Sydney.

I remember being in our backyard one day. There was a beautiful apple tree lush with fragrant white blossoms and the sky was a cerulean blue. I knew the scene was vibrant with color, but I couldn't see it that way. It was as though I were wearing glasses that turned everything gray. *What's wrong with me?* I wondered, slumping against the tree. Maybe I was tired. We had two children by then and another on the way. Living abroad was exhausting. I needed more rest. Rest was the answer.

So began a pattern that lasted thirty years. In the mornings I was with the children and ran errands, but every afternoon I retreated to my bedroom for a nap. As we moved from country to country the naps became longer. In hot tropical locales it seemed perfectly justifiable. In Mexico the afternoon siesta was part of the culture. But what I could never admit to a soul was that I looked forward to that nap more than time with the children or Jim. The best part of the day was when I got to shut the world out for an hour or two.

Maybe I'll feel better in the next place we live, I'd tell myself. *Maybe a different house will help. Or a different country.* "You're so fortunate," my mother wrote to me. Of course I was. I was truly blessed. I owed it to God to be grateful. Why didn't I feel grateful? Maybe God could help me.

So I turned to the Bible. The Psalms in particular gave language to my bleakness: "Therefore is my spirit overwhelmed within me; my heart within me is desolate."

I read that Bible cover to cover again and again. In different countries we joined different churches—Baptist, Congregational, Presbyterian—and I went to Bible studies. I grew confident in my command of Scripture but not in my capacity to feel joy, contentment, pleasure.

It was a relief to return to the United States for good in 1979 after seventeen years abroad. We settled in New Jersey and one by one our children went off to college. Here where I wasn't a stranger anymore, I couldn't think of what to say to the other mothers at the supermarket. I hurried home after meetings at church. One afternoon I was getting a snack for Jon, our youngest. "Mom," he said, "how was your day?" *Just as gray as all the days before, one day like the next,* I thought. Yet I couldn't tell my son how I really felt. I couldn't ever tell anyone.

"Great," I said, smiling automatically.

That Father's Day, Jim's dad joined us for the weekend. The older kids all came home from college and we went out to a nice restaurant. Jim's dad was telling the kids about something he'd done in the war. Jennifer, our eldest daughter, turned to me and said, "Mom, what about you? You've never told us much about your father." I started to say something. But the words got caught somewhere inside of me. I looked around at my children, who looked back at me quizzically. All at once I lost control. I sobbed like a child, cried like I hadn't cried in I don't know how long. I stood up, hiding my face behind my hands. "I'm sorry," I said, "I'm so sorry." I quickly excused myself.

The experience was mortifying. How dare I ruin Father's Day with my crying! I promised myself it would never happen again. I had a perfect life. Why the tears? Then one Monday morning I had an appointment with our pastor. I was debating a point of Scripture with him. He looked at me and paused, "Marianne, what's really going on with you? How are you feeling?" The same awful thing happened that had happened on Father's Day. I burst into deep, convulsive sobs. What on earth was wrong with me?

"I don't know what's come over me," I said, trying to get control of myself. "I'm really so sorry."

"Are you sad about something, Marianne?" he asked gently.

"I have no right to be," I protested. "I have every reason to be happy."

"Marianne, you need someone to help you. Have you ever thought about seeing a therapist?" Before I could protest, my pastor shocked me. He had seen one himself, and it had helped him address issues beyond his control. A therapist? A minister seeing a therapist?

"But I don't need that," I said. "I speak to God. I tell him everything."

"God also gives us people to help us deal with our troubles."

Fearful that saying anything about the past would be disloyal to my mother and father, I went to see a therapist. Week after week I talked. And finally, I talked about how I really felt. I relived that night my father told me not to cry. I remembered waiting for Poppi to come home from the war. I was brave. I didn't cry.

"What happened," the therapist explained, "is that you put a lid on all your emotions." The naps, the sense of worthlessness, the fear of others—they were symptoms of depression. Yes, I had buried my sorrow. Yet with it I'd buried my joy. I'd tried to extinguish any feelings as wrong or weak. It was in that emotional soil that depression took root.

In two years of therapy, I cried and talked—and even laughed. I didn't have to fake my emotions. I felt whole, connected to myself and to God more deeply than ever.

The more I learned about depression, the more I yearned to help others. I became a therapist myself. Now I have a private practice with an office in a church building, which makes it easier for some clients to talk about God. I can tell them how prayer and the Bible gave me comfort but couldn't replace the professional treatment my illness required. That's how God helped me most.

I turn to my Bible for encouragement and I pray more than ever, but more often my prayers are words of praise and thanksgiving. Of joy. Along with the psalmist I can say, "The Lord brought me out of darkness and the deepest gloom and broke away the chains."

The game of life is not so much in holding a good hand as playing a poor hand well.
—H. T. LESLIE

THE SECOND TUESDAY WE TALK ABOUT FEELING SORRY FOR YOURSELF

MITCH ALBOM

A came back the next Tuesday. And for many Tuesdays that followed. I looked forward to these visits more than one would think, considering I was flying seven hundred miles to sit alongside a dying man. But I seemed to slip into a time warp when I visited Morrie, and I liked myself better when I was there. I no longer rented a cellular phone for the rides from the airport. *Let them wait,* I told myself, mimicking Morrie.

The newspaper situation in Detroit had not improved. In fact, it had grown increasingly insane, with nasty confrontations between picketers and replacement workers, people arrested, beaten, lying in the street in front of delivery trucks.

In light of this, my visits with Morrie felt like a cleansing rinse of human kindness. We talked about life and we talked about love. We talked about one of Morrie's favorite subjects, compassion, and why our society had such a shortage of it. Before my third visit, I stopped at a market called Bread and Circus—I had seen their bags in Morrie's house and figured he must like the food there—and I loaded up with plastic containers from their fresh food take-away, things like vermicelli with vegetables and carrot soup and baklava.

When I entered Morrie's study, I lifted the bags as if I'd just robbed a bank.

"Food man!" I bellowed.

Morrie rolled his eyes and smiled.

Meanwhile, I looked for signs of the disease's progression. His fingers worked well enough to write with a pencil, or hold up his glasses, but he could not lift his arms much higher than his chest. He was spending less and less time in the kitchen or living room and more in his study, where he had a large reclining chair set up with pillows, blankets, and specially cut pieces of foam rubber that held his feet and gave support to his withered legs. He kept a bell near his side, and when his head needed adjusting or he had to "go on the commode," as he referred to it, he would shake the bell and Connie, Tony, Bertha, or Amy—his small army of home care workers would come in. It wasn't always easy for him to lift the bell, and he got frustrated when he couldn't make it work.

I asked Morrie if he felt sorry for himself.

"Sometimes, in the mornings," he said. "That's when I mourn. I feel around my body, I move my fingers and my hands—whatever I can still move—and I mourn what I've lost. I mourn the slow, insidious way in which I'm dying. But then I stop mourning."

Just like that?

"I give myself a good cry if I need it. But then I concentrate on all the good things still in my life. On the people who are coming to see me. On the stories I'm going to hear. On you—if it's Tuesday. Because we're Tuesday people."

I grinned. Tuesday people.

"Mitch, I don't allow myself any more self-pity than that. A little each morning, a few tears, and that's all."

I thought about all the people I knew who spent many of their waking hours feeling sorry for themselves. How useful it would be to put a daily limit on self-pity. Just a few tearful minutes, then on with the day. And if Morrie could do it, with such a horrible disease . . .

"It's only horrible if you see it that way," Morrie said. "It's horrible to watch my body slowly wilt away to nothing. But it's also wonderful because of all the time I get to say good-bye."

He smiled. "Not everyone is so lucky."

I studied him in his chair, unable to stand, to wash, to pull on his pants. Lucky? Did he really say lucky?

> *There are two ways of meeting difficulties:*
> *you alter the difficulties, or you alter yourself to meet them.*
> —Phyllis Bottome

I Thought I Had a Handle on Life, But Then It Fell Off

Barbara Johnson

Did you ever see that episode of *I Love Lucy* where Lucy gets stuck in the freezer and can't get the door open? When she finally emerges, she has icicles dangling off her nose, her head, and her elbows, and her clothes are frozen solid. I thought of that silly image when a friend of mine, the PTA president at her daughter's school, told me about a nightmare experience she had recently when she was helping serve soft drinks during the school's annual field day.

All day long the dedicated PTA mothers worked outside in the blistering heat of a June day in Florida, hurriedly pouring drinks for the sweltering students, who flocked to the booth for refreshments after competing in the various events.

At one point my friend, Sue, was dispatched to the school's kitchen to get another bag of ice. No one was in the kitchen, but she found the massive, six-inch-thick door of the huge, walk-in freezer, stepped inside, and flipped on the light.

It felt so good in the freezer after spending several hours in the ninety-degree heat that, even though she was in a hurry, Sue stopped a moment to close her eyes and soak in the sweet coolness of the frosty air. Then she found the ice and turned toward the door.

"My heart stopped," she said. "There was no handle on the door! It was just a big, smooth, metal slab set into the wall. I couldn't imagine how I could get out. I tried to get my fingers in the crack between the door and the wall so I could pull on the door, but it fit too tightly. Then I saw a little lever on the wall next to the door. I shoved the lever up and down, thinking it might somehow open the door, but nothing happened—absolutely nothing.

"I exploded into full-bore panic. I thought how ironic it was going to be to freeze to death on such a hot day. I wondered how long it would be before any of the other mothers missed me—and how long it took to die in a freezer.

"Even though I knew no one was in the kitchen, I started shouting for help and rapping on the door with my knuckles, screaming to make myself heard. I figured at least the exertion might keep me warm for a little while.

"Suddenly the door swung inward and nearly knocked me down. The custodian stood there with this strange look on his face. I was so relieved I burst into tears and said, 'Oh, thank you, thank you, thank you! I was so scared!'

"He looked at me with that same strange look and said, 'Why? What happened?'

"I said excitedly, 'I couldn't get the door open. There's no handle!'

"The custodian smiled a gentle little smile and motioned for me to step back into the freezer. He came in with me, and then he gave the door the smallest little push, and it easily swung outward. 'Look,' he said, 'it's a swinging door. You don't need a handle—you just push.'"

A lot of hurting parents know exactly how it feels to find themselves frozen in "full-bore panic" with no means of escape. What a blessing it is, then, to have someone come alongside us and show us a simple way out of our misery.

That's what I want to do—share some of the ideas that other parents have used to find their way off the ceiling, up from the pit, through the fire—or out of the freezer. Sometimes the ideas seem simple—like a gentle push on a swinging door. . . .

There is a thin line that separates laughter and pain, comedy and tragedy, humor and hurt. And how do you know laughter if there is no pain to compare it with? . . .

Sometimes it seems we're unable to cross that line from pain to joy because we can't see the line! Our lives are too cluttered with painful experiences to even know it's there. If that's your situation . . . let go! Turn loose!

Bruce Larson tells a story about a man who was taking a cruise on an ocean liner. Somehow one of his socks got away from him and blew over the railing, forever lost. Without a thought, the man flipped the other sock over the railing too, then stretched out on the chaise lounge and took a nap. He knew when he was looking at a hopeless situation, and he wasn't about to let it ruin his opportunity for pleasure.

In contrast, many of us would take the remaining sock home and KEEP it, hoping a mate might miraculously turn up sometime. But all we would be doing is cluttering up our sock drawer. Instead, like the man on the ship, we need to let go of the painful situations that are out of our control and step out, unencumbered, knowing God holds our future in His hands.

Our lives can become so cluttered with all the stuff we insist on hanging on to—both physical (like single socks and broken gadgets) and emotional (like guilt and pain and misery). I saw a little essay by an unknown writer that described all the stuff that clutters our lives: closet stuff, drawer stuff, attic stuff, basement stuff, good stuff, bad stuff, food stuff, cleaning stuff, medicine stuff, clothes stuff, outside stuff, stuff to make us smell better and look younger, stuff to make us look healthier, stuff to hold us in or fill us out, stuff to read, stuff to play with, stuff to entertain us, little stuff, big stuff, useful stuff, and junky stuff.

The essay ends with this happy reminder: "Now when we leave all our stuff and go to heaven, whatever happens to our stuff won't matter. We will still have the good stuff God has prepared for us in heaven."

*Our grand business is not to see what lies dimly at a distance,
but to do what lies clearly at hand.*
—THOMAS CARLYLE

DON'T SECOND-GUESS GOD

HEATHER WHITESTONE

*A*n early 1996, right before John and I were married, I was invited to travel to Taiwan and speak about deaf issues. I had never been to Asia, and so was thrilled to have the opportunity to travel overseas. My trip was sponsored by Citibank's "With Your Heart You Can Hear the Whole World" charity drive, and the bank worked with the Taipei city government to promote early detection and intervention programs. As I walked through the buildings and schools of Taipei, I was greeted with the universal "I love you" sign that made me feel at home.

Taiwan is an extremely modern and beautiful country, but when I entered the deaf community there, I felt as though I had traveled back to the nineteenth century. The prevailing cultural opinion holds that deaf people cannot have a normal life, and so few deaf Taiwanese people have more than a second-grade education. I visited one deaf school that did have computers, but the students were playing games with them, not really learning how to speak. I asked if they had learned to write, and was told that the deaf students were treated as if they were learning-impaired.

I was shocked. I talked about my STARS program (an interpreter signed for the audience), but the students looked at me blankly as if they didn't understand. Then

The gladness of the heart is the life of man,
and the joyfulness of a man prolongeth his days.
—SIRACH 30:22

THE TURNING POINT OF MY LIFE

A. J. CRONIN

A was thirty-three at the time, a doctor in the West End of London. I had been lucky in advancing through several arduous Welsh mining assistantships to my own practice—acquired on the installment plan from a dear old family physician who at our first interview, gazed at my cracked boots and frayed cuffs, and trusted me.

I think I wasn't a bad doctor. My patients seemed to like me—not only the nice old ladies with nothing wrong with them, who lived near the Park and paid handsomely for my cheerful bedside manner, but the cabbies, porters and deadbeats in the mews and back streets of Bayswater, who paid nothing and often had a great deal wrong with them.

Yet there was something . . . though I treated everything that came my way, read all the medical journals, attended scientific meetings, and even found time to take complex post-graduate diplomas . . . I wasn't quite sure of myself. I didn't stick at anything for long. I had successive ideas of specializing in dermatology, in aural surgery, in pediatrics, but discarded them all. While I worked all day and half of most nights, I really lacked perseverance, stability.

One day I developed indigestion. After resisting my wife's entreaties for several weeks, I went casually to consult a friendly colleague. I expected a bottle of bismuth

and an invitation to bridge. I received instead the shock of my life: a sentence to six months' complete rest in the country on a milk diet. I had a gastric ulcer.

The place of exile, chosen after excruciating contention, was a small farmhouse near the village of Tarbert in the Scottish Highlands. Imagine a lonely whitewashed steading set on a rain-drenched loch amid ferocious mountains rising into gray mist, with long-horned cattle, like elders of the kirk, sternly munching thistles in the foreground. That was Fyne Farm. Conceive of a harassed stranger in city clothes arriving with a pain in his middle and a box of peptonizing powders in his suitcase. That was I.

Nothing is more agonizing to the active man than enforced idleness. A week of Fyne Farm drove me crazy. Debarred from all physical pursuits, I was reduced to feeding the chickens and learning to greet the disapproving cattle by their Christian names. Casting around desperately for something to do, I had a sudden idea. For years, at the back of my mind, I had nursed the vague illusion that I might write. Often, indeed, in unguarded moments, I had remarked to my wife, "You know, I believe I could write a novel if I had time," at which she would smile kindly across her knitting, murmur, "Do you, dear?" and tactfully lead me back to talk of Johnnie Smith's whooping cough.

Now, as I stood on the shore of that desolate Highland loch I raised my voice in a surge of self-justification: "By Heavens! This is my opportunity. Gastric ulcer or no gastric ulcer, I will write a novel." Before I could change my mind I walked straight to the village and bought myself two dozen penny exercise books.

Upstairs in my cold, clean bedroom was a scrubbed deal table and a very hard chair. Next morning I found myself in this chair, facing a new exercise book open upon the table, slowly becoming aware that, short of dog-Latin prescriptions, I had never composed a significant phrase in all my life. It was a discouraging thought as I picked up my pen and gazed out the window. Never mind, I would begin. Three

hours later Mrs. Angus, the farmer's wife, called me to dinner. The page was still blank.

As I went down to my milk and junket—they call this "curds" in Tarbert—I felt a dreadful fool. I recollected, rather grimly, the sharp advice with which my old schoolmaster had goaded me to action. "Get it down!" he had said. "If it stops in your head it will always be nothing. Get it down." And so, after lunch, I went upstairs and began to get it down.

Perhaps the tribulations of the next three months are best omitted. I had in my head clear enough the theme I wished to treat—the tragic record of a man's egoism and bitter pride. I even had the title of the book. But beyond these naive fundamentals I was lamentably unprepared. I had no pretensions to technique, no knowledge of style or form. I had never seen a thesaurus. The difficulty of simple statement staggered me. I spent hours looking for an adjective. I corrected and recorrected until the page looked like a spider's web, then I tore it up and started all over again.

Yet once I had begun, the thing haunted me. My characters took shape, spoke to me, laughed, wept, excited me. When an idea struck me in the middle of the night I would get up, light a candle, and sprawl on the floor until I had translated it to paper. At first my rate of progress was some eight hundred labored words a day. By the end of the second month it was a ready two thousand.

Suddenly, when I was halfway through, the inevitable happened. Desolation struck me like an avalanche. I asked myself: "Why am I wearing myself out with this toil for which I am so preposterously ill-equipped?" I threw down my pen. Feverishly, I read over the first chapters which had just arrived in typescript from my secretary in London. I was appalled. Never, never had I seen such nonsense in all my life. No one would read it. I saw, finally, that I was a presumptuous lunatic, that all I had written, all that I could ever write was wasted effort, sheer

futility. Abruptly, furiously, I bundled up the manuscript, went out and threw it in the ash can.

Drawing a sullen satisfaction from my surrender or, as I preferred to phrase it, my return to sanity, I went for a walk in the drizzling rain. Halfway down the loch shore I came upon old Angus, the farmer, patiently and laboriously ditching a patch of the bogged and peaty heath which made up the bulk of his hard-won little croft. As I drew near, he gazed up at me in some surprise: he knew of my intention and, with that inborn Scottish reverence for "letters," had tacitly approved it. When I told him what I had just done, and why, his weathered face slowly changed, his keen blue eyes scanned me with disappointment and a queer contempt. He was a silent man and it was long before he spoke. Even then his words were cryptic.

"No doubt you're the one that's right, doctor, and I'm the one that's wrong . . . ." He seemed to look right to the bottom of me. "My father ditched this bog all his days and never made a pasture. I've dug it all *my* days and I've never made a pasture. But pasture or no pasture," he placed his foot dourly on the spade, "I canna help but dig. For my father knew and I know that if you only dig enough a pasture can be made here."

I understood. I watched his dogged working figure with rising anger and resentment. I was resentful because he had what I had not: a terrible stubbornness to see the job through at all costs, an unquenchable flame of resolution brought to the simplest, the most arid duties of life. And suddenly my trivial dilemma became magnified, transmuted, until it stood as the timeless problem of all mortality—the comfortable retreat, or the arduous advance without prospect of reward.

I tramped back to the farm, drenched, shamed, furious, and picked the soggy bundle from the ash can. I dried it in the kitchen oven. Then I flung it on the table and set to work again with a kind of frantic desperation. I lost myself in the ferociousness of my purpose. I would not be beaten, I would not give in. I wrote

harder than ever. At last, toward the end of the third month, I wrote *finis*. The relief, the sense of emancipation, was unbelievable. I had kept my word. I had created a book. Whether it was good, bad, or indifferent I did not care.

I chose a publisher by the simple expedient of closing my eyes and pricking a catalogue with a pin. I dispatched the completed manuscript and promptly forgot about it.

In the days which followed I gradually regained my health, and I began to chafe at idleness. I wanted to be back in harness.

At last the date of my deliverance drew near. I went around the village saying good-by to the simple folk who had become my friends. As I entered the post office, the postmaster presented me with a telegram—an urgent invitation to meet the publisher. I took it straight away and showed it, without a word, to John Angus.

The novel I had thrown away was chosen by the Book Society, dramatized and serialized, translated into nineteen languages, bought by Hollywood. It has sold millions of copies. It altered my life radically, beyond my wildest dreams . . . and all because of a timely lesson in the grace of perseverance.

But that lesson goes deeper still. Today, when the air resounds with shrill defeatist cries, when half our stricken world is wailing in discouragement: "What is the use . . . to work . . . to save . . . to go on living . . . with Armageddon round the corner?" I am glad to recollect it. The door is wide open to darkness and despair. The way to close that door is to go on doing whatever job we are doing, and to finish it.

The virtue of all achievement, as known to my old Scots farmer, is victory over oneself. Those who know this victory can never know defeat.

A merry heart doeth good like a medicine:
but a broken spirit drieth the bones.
—PROVERBS 17:22

THE SNOOPY FACTOR

RICHARD H. SCHNEIDER

Along with the rest of the world, I mourned the death of Charles Schulz last year. I could hardly imagine starting my day without seeing the antics of Snoopy in my morning paper. But I took comfort in the memory of my interview with Schulz almost twenty years ago. On that sunny day in Santa Rosa, California, we sat in the stands of the town ice rink, and Schulz told me about his recovery from open-heart surgery. "There I was in the hospital, feeling just awful, and the nurse kept insisting I draw something on the wall of my room.

"For days I stared at the blank wall," he went on, "while doctors checked my charts and nurses urged me to blow in this plastic inhalator that was supposed to help keep my lungs clear. I tried, but it was almost impossible to get enough breath to keep the little plastic balls inside floating. I was feeling fed up until it dawned on me that this was the picture I'd draw on the wall."

On his fifth night in the hospital, Schulz got out of bed, took up the black marker that had been left for him, and drew cartoons of Snoopy blowing into a miniature inhalator of his own. He returned to bed feeling much better.

Years later I found myself in a hospital bed feeling grouchy and miserable. I'd had heart surgery, and my nurses kept waking me up and asking me to blow into a

plastic inhalator. It was almost impossible to keep all the balls floating. That's when I remembered Schulz. I could picture Snoopy blowing into the inhalator and I started laughing like I hadn't laughed in days. I felt so much better afterward. Almost ready to write on walls.

Laughter is wonderful medicine. That Charles Schulz was able to take his own struggles and turn them into humor was often mentioned in the obituaries about him. I'd like to add that there was one Bible verse he truly took to heart: A merry heart doeth good like a medicine: but a broken spirit drieth the bones. (Proverbs 17:22).

*One of the secrets of life is making
stepping stones out of stumbling blocks.*
—JACK PENN

FEAR AND JOY

PAMELA KENNEDY

We recently moved—again. In the past twenty-eight years, we have moved eighteen times, so perhaps moving shouldn't be traumatic for our family. But there are always unknown aspects of new locations, schools, neighborhoods, even cultures that set our hearts to beating just a bit faster. Will the children adjust? Will we make friends quickly? Will we find good dentists and doctors and a beautician who knows how to cut my hair the way I like? Some of the concerns are big ones and others quite small, but they often join together to form a degree of fear that accompanies us to our new home. Mixed with that apprehension is another feeling equally as familiar: the anticipation and joy of discovery. For each new location holds, like an unopened gift, the promise of delightful surprises, exciting adventures, and enriching friendships.

As I reread the Easter story from Matthew's Gospel, I see that same mixture of fear and joy in the hearts of the women who hurried to the tomb that first Easter dawn. They were met, not with the expected rocky sepulcher containing the body of their Lord, but an angel who told them Jesus had risen and was headed to Galilee! Everything they knew about death and dying, about tombs and bodies, was turned upside down in that moment. They moved from a comfortable understanding about the world to a new and uncomfortable revelation that left them both fearful and filled with joy.

I believe their fear came from the changes that confronted them. What would happen now? Would anyone believe their experience with the angel? How would this new revelation alter their lives? These questions, just like mine about moving to a new location and all the readjustments involved in relocating our family, held a degree of fear because the answers were hidden. This was uncharted territory. But notice the women's fear was accompanied by joy. It was a joy driven by the information they received from the angel—"And go quickly, and tell his disciples that he (Jesus) is risen from the dead; and, behold, he goeth before you into Galilee; there shall ye see him" (Matthew 28:7).

Although I may not receive an angelic revelation, I can participate in the same joy these first-century believers experienced when I understand the truth that Jesus is still alive and he goes before me. Meditating on his comforting and encouraging presence, I need not fear the unknown future. True, I do not know what lies ahead, but I know the One who goes before me and waits for me there. My anxious expectations turn to bright hope as I trust in God to be present in my future as surely as he has been in my past. In his abiding strength and power, I find the courage needed to face the future, to make new friends, to start a new job, to discover new abilities— even to find a new hairdresser!

Some of us may never move to a new location, but all of us experience changes that bring us face to face with the unknown. Understanding that God has already gone on ahead brings joy even in the midst of our fear. In that assurance we can start down the path before us, just as the women did that long ago Easter morning when they hurried into their future, afraid, yet filled with joy.

We seek the comfort of another . . . Someone to help us
through the never-ending attempt to understand ourselves.
And in the end, someone to comfort us along the way.
—MARLIN FINCH LUPUS

INTO THIN MUD

ANNE LAMOTT

*I*t's funny where we look for salvation, and where we actually find it. . . .

When I was a kid and my father got depressed, we all frantically tried to pump him out of it. The theory was that if Dad was OK, there would be trickle-down, and everyone's needs would be met. But if Dad was not OK, we were all doomed. So this has always been my first line of attack against a slump: start pumping.

I ate a few chocolates and felt more animated. Then I crashed and was just as sad as I'd been before, but fatter and more tired.

The next morning I stayed in bed quite late, not wanting to get up. I remembered lying in bed as a child, pretending to have paralyzed legs as the result of my heroic effort to save a baby from a kidnapper, or fire, or wolves. I figured that if you had suffered a wound or handicap in an act of self-sacrifice, people would not only see how badly you felt but would also believe that you were worthy of tender care. So I was lying in bed trying to drag myself into a sitting position when my friend Neshama called. She suggested we go for a hike. I could not think of a single thing I

felt less like doing. *A hike? And me in my condition?* But Neshama seems to think I am worthy of tender care even when I am at my most ridiculous, so I said I would go.

Neshama and I go back twenty-five years. We've been through births, deaths, estrangements, confusions, and just about everything life can deal out, and have maintained our friendship through it all. Part of our bond is having had fuzzy-haired bookworm childhoods. Also she is one of the few people I know who can tolerate a lot of silence and stillness; they are central to her spirituality, as is the joy she finds in music and dance. She loves God in the guise of kindness and nature, although she calls God "Howard," as in "Our Father, who art in heaven, Howard be thy name."

On this morning, I put on the nicest possible clothes in an effort to raise my spirits. I wore a white linen blouse, and sandals, and lipstick. An hour later Neshama and I were walking down a hillside toward a marsh we had spotted from the road. From up above it looked fertile and abandoned, surrounded by nondescript suburban houses and anonymous buildings, like Mesopotamia accidentally deposited in the midst of a military complex. You felt that no one living there was even aware of the marsh. It also looked quite boggy, like maybe you should be wearing waders instead of sandals, but I figured, [well]—this must be where we were going because this was where we were.

We left the road where the hillside dipped down into the marsh, a brackish tidal channel with lots of red pickerelweed and cattails. A dirt path ran alongside it. There were snowy egrets in the channel, with star-shaped yellow feet. Everything was very quiet. Even though the freeway was not far away, you could hear only white noise and soft rustle, as if the marsh had sucked up all the other sound. Sometimes you'd hear a grackly crow noise or one of the egrets, who tend to sound as if they need oiling.

We walked along the path until we got to a thin ribbon of water flowing out from the channel toward the bay. I stopped, remembering the Sunday not long ago when Mary Williams testified. She brought a long pole and an old housedress

draped over her arm, blue, faded, and frayed. At the point when Veronica would normally begin the sermon, she instead asked Mary to stand and tell us her baptism story. Mary rose with the help of the women who sat beside her, and while she spoke, they spotted her, like you would a gymnast.

She put the housedress on over her church clothes to represent the robe she wore to be baptized in. She tugged it into place and picked up her pole. Then, her voice as soft and rough and Southern as biscuits, she told of the day seventy years before when she stepped into the Mississippi River to be baptized. She lived in Louisiana. She was not yet in her teens and her mother had been dead for years. On the morning of her baptism, she went with her father and brother to the river. There was a ring of poles sticking out of the water near the shore. The deacons had walked out in the river that morning, feeling around on the muddy floor with their poles until they found a solid patch of riverbed. Then they stuck the sticks into the mud, forming a circle in which the people could safely stand with their pastor and be baptized.

She tapped the linoleum at our church like a blind woman with a white stick, the eyes of that girl still right there in that walnut face.

And suddenly at the marsh with Neshama, the ground and vegetation at our feet began to get a little watery, and then we began to hear sucking noises, swampy quicksandy sucking noises, and pretty soon my overpriced walking sandals had been swallowed up by mud.

We moved as quickly as possible through the bog to drier ground on the other side. Then we stared down at our muddy shoes, and we started to laugh. It's just *mud*, we realized. It washes off. Mary Williams got baptized in it. So we tromped on until the path came smack-dab up to a stumpy wet slope, with ratty little shrubs growing out of it. The path picked up again at the top. There was nothing to do but to scale it, and I use "scale" loosely here, since the slope was only about three feet tall.

"Let me help you there, little lady," I said. "I'll go up first and then give you a hand." So I planted a foot on the muddy dune, grasped a root, and would have pulled myself up the hill nicely if the root had held. But it didn't. It pulled up out of the slope, and I slid down on my backside to the wet ground. Both of us started to laugh. Then I got up and tried again and this time I made it up. Planting one foot firmly on the driest ground I could find, I reached back down for Neshama's hand.

"Is this a good idea?" she asked. "Are you braced?"

"Yes," I insisted and pulled her toward me, and she lifted up off the ground and moved upward a couple of feet, until I started sliding back down toward her and we both landed noisily in the mud.

I looked at her. She was wearing a blue linen dress and ballet slippers because she was going to work from here, and she was utterly covered with silt. I started to laugh. It was odd to be so old and to have gotten so muddy, to have such dirty drawers and no angry parents around, and no more face to save.

I was laughing so hard that I felt maniacal and not at all sure that I wasn't about to cry. But I felt like air was bubbling into a place inside me that hadn't been getting much lately. I looked at Neshama's ballet slippers. "Boy," I said, "are you going to get it when Mom sees you," and she nodded. I couldn't stop laughing. It made me feel helpless in the best possible way. The laughter rose from way below, from below my feet, from underneath me in the mud.

Finally we stopped laughing, wiped our eyes, sighed, gathered some composure. We sat there silently for a long time. There were egrets on a telephone wire above us, looking down on the smorgasbord of wiggly jumpy things that lived in the shallow water; maybe birds like to get up high so they can see if there are food patterns in the swamp. And there were two blackbirds on the wire, sitting on either side of the egrets like bookends. The air smelled of dry grasses—warm smells, a little like a Laundromat.

Then I let my head drop down narcoleptically and closed my eyes for a while.

Against the sparkly black screen behind my eyes, all these people appeared, like people in a come-as-you-are fashion show, strangers to each other but beloved by me. There were all the sick little kids we know, and all the friends who had died—Mimi and Ken Nelson and Mary Williams—and the old people in my family and church who had grown so suddenly frail, and the man with whom I used to be in love and who used to be in love with me. And I thought to myself, *Well, no wonder you're this sad.* The silence of the marsh was so profound that it could have been the flip side of the singing in my church. Just last Sunday the people of St. Andrew had sung the old spiritual, "Go Down, Moses," *a cappella* because the pianist was gone, and a bunch of people were crying, singing very loudly with their eyes closed, and the singing of that cry of a song was a wonderful form of communion. How come you can hear a chord, and then another chord, and then your heart breaks open?

When Neshama and I finally got up to go, I was still sad, but better. This is the most profound spiritual truth I know: that even when we're most sure that love can't conquer all, it seems to anyway. It goes down into the rat hole with us, in the guise of our friends, and there it swells and comforts. It gives us second winds, third winds, hundredth winds. It struck me that I have spent so much time trying to pump my way into feeling the solace I used to feel in my parents' arms. But pumping always fails you in the end. The truth is that your spirits don't rise until you get way down. Maybe it's because this—the mud, the bottom—is where it all rises from. Maybe without it, whatever rises would fly off or evaporate before you could even be with it for a moment. But when someone enters that valley with you, that mud, it somehow saves you again. At the marsh, all that mud and one old friend worked like a tenderizing mallet. Where before there had been tough fibers, hardness, and held breath, now there were mud, dirt, water, air, mess—and I felt soft and clean.

Life is God's novel. Let him write it.
—ISAAC BASHEVIS SINGER

MOMENTS OF GRACE

JOHN SHERRILL

The traffic from our home to New York's Penn Station had been bumper to bumper all the way. Arriving with barely twenty minutes to spare before my mother's train to Kentucky departed, I circled the station anxiously, looking for a parking place. No porter was in sight and there was no way Mother could wrestle her heavy suitcase to the train by herself.

"Please, Lord, a place to park!"

I must have said the prayer out loud because Mother exclaimed, "I'm surprised at you, John! You don't really believe God hands out parking places!"

She had barely gotten the words out when, half a block up, a car pulled away from the curb.

"You know perfectly well that was a coincidence," Mother insisted as I hauled the suitcase from the trunk. "Why, nothing annoyed your father more than what he called 'convenience miracles.'"

That space opening up was probably just a bit of fortunate timing. Still, after I had seen Mother safely aboard and started the drive home, I thought about what she had said. Mother—and Dad when he was alive—believed God was involved in daily life. It was egoism they objected to, someone imagining a world orchestrated for his personal comfort. I heartily agreed, and yet certain fragile events in my life hinted at a different view. Not one of them was earthshaking, but each of them made me glad.

I remembered one morning some years ago: My wife, Tib, and I were eating breakfast when a wail came from upstairs. "That's the contact-lens cry," Tib said. We went up and found our daughter Liz on her hands and knees, combing through the orange shag rug in her bedroom. Tib and I joined the search, to no avail. Half an hour later Liz left for her summer job wearing her "awful" glasses.

Tib and I continued looking. In the sheets and blankets, in the rug in the upstairs bathroom, everywhere. A replacement lens would use a good deal of what Liz had made toward college expenses by wrapping meat at the A&P. Returning in defeat to the breakfast table, we decided that if the loss mattered to Liz, it mattered to God.

"Father," I began, "you know where that lens is and you know what it means to Liz. Will you please—"

I had gotten no farther than that when Tib sprang up from her chair and left the room. A minute later she called softly, "John . . ."

She had lifted the stopper from the washbasin in the downstairs bathroom. And there, clinging to the bottom of that shiny metal cylinder, was a teardrop of clear plastic.

"Why did you think to come here?" I asked, after I found my voice.

"I didn't think," Tib said. "My feet just took me here."

My mother, I thought as the traffic inched northward, might have called that a coincidence too. But suppose Mother was wrong. Suppose this sort of experience is part of God's wooing of us, inviting us to live in a world where events constantly mesh and intermesh like notes in a symphony.

I am more than a little claustrophobic. I've been known to vault over seats in minivans to escape that confined, doorless space in the rear, and I once had to postpone getting a CAT scan, so powerful was the fear of being enclosed inside that machine's narrow tunnel.

A month ago I boarded a plane for Nashville just as a voice on the loudspeaker was asking people to find their places as soon as possible. "We have a full flight today, and we cannot push back until everyone is seated."

I worked my way down the crowded aisle to the window seat I had requested. It was in the last row—and there was no window. Momentarily I froze with apprehension. Then, taking a deep breath, I ducked beneath the overhead storage bin and squeezed my six-foot frame into a space that seemed designed for toddlers. My knees were jammed under my chin; the seat would not recline. The man beside me had just reseated himself when I jack-in-the-boxed up, right over him and into the aisle. "Sorry!" I apologized.

"I can't handle this," I told the flight attendant who hurried back to see what the trouble was.

She tried to help me. "Maybe," she said, raising her voice, "someone would be willing to change places with you?" Nearby passengers seemed suddenly absorbed in their reading. The voice on the loudspeaker asked again for everyone to be seated. I said a silent prayer that was more like an inner scream: *Help!*

Seconds later another attendant, perhaps twenty rows forward, raised his hand. Somehow, on this fully booked flight, a seat had opened up—a seat on the aisle. As I slid into it, the woman in the window seat clutched my arm.

"Oh, thank goodness!" she said. "I was so afraid no one would be sitting next to me. I promise I won't talk during the flight, but, please, would you talk to me while we take off? I've never flown before and I'm terrified!"

I did talk to her, not only confessing my own irrational fear, but, as she told me when we arrived in Nashville, relieving hers as well. Who was it who called coincidence "catching the universe in the act of rhyming"?

Mother's objection to my parking-place prayer would be warranted if I ever

found myself feeling entitled to such divine poetry. But most of these grace-filled moments, in my experience, are not even asked for. I'll never forget the morning when Tib took her new bird-watcher's binoculars out of their case for the first time. Experimenting, she tried to bring the clothesline in our backyard into focus. "I must be doing it wrong," she said. "All I'm getting is a blue blur."

Tib twisted the wheel again. The blur turned out to be an indigo bunting, perched on the particular inch of line where Tib had "randomly" pointed the glasses. Never before, or in the twenty-six years since, have we spotted another of those tiny jewel-like birds in our yard. But bird-watching has been Tib's joy ever since that initial piece of exquisitely composed timing.

These little convergences are sprinkled throughout the everyday lives of each of us. When they occur, we usually thank something. We'll thank goodness, or our lucky stars, or even burst out with a "Thank God," not really meaning it.

But why not mean it? These experiences are like the grace notes that appear from time to time in the music I sing with our church choir. Grace notes are written small, ornamenting the melody line. They are not necessary to the music; they're there to add gaiety, brightness, delight.

Grace notes seem to be written into our lives as well—unessential yet welcome gifts. From now on I'll choose to regard them as small miracles granted not for convenience, but for joy, and I'll remember that the meaning of the word grace is "thanks."

So much sadness exists in the world that we are all under obligation to contribute as much joy as lies within our powers.
—JOHN SUTHERLAND BONNELL

ANGEL MOON

LAELE CRUIKSHANK

There's something about the moon that just seems to draw my family. It started with my grandmother Gertrude. She loved to take me outside when I was a girl to look up at the night sky. I'd tilt my head back and listen fascinated as she told me about all the different heavenly bodies. But the moon was her favorite.

One night, looking back and forth across the sky, I couldn't find the moon anywhere, though we'd seen it just a few days before.

"Where's the moon tonight, Grandma?"

"That's how the moon works, darling," she'd explained. "Some nights it's there for us to see, and others it isn't. But it's never really gone. Even when we can't see it at all, it's still there in the heavens, looking over us—just like God is."

Todd, the older of my two sons, caught Grandma's love of the moon too. She took him out when he was little like she had with me, and he hung on her every word. When I drove him home from his late-afternoon piano lessons, we made a game of watching the eastern sky and waiting for the first glimpse of the moon rising through the trees. The most special times were when it came up full.

I bought Todd a calendar with the phases of the moon on it when he went off for his first year at the University of New Hampshire. The university was only forty

minutes away, and Todd came home plenty of weekends. But his dad, Rob, his younger brother, Scott, and I were still glad to see summer arrive and Todd back home full-time.

The August morning when Todd was packing to leave for his second year at UNH, I got a sudden, powerful urge to have some time alone with him. "Want to go have a picnic by the pool?" I asked. "Just for an hour—so we can talk a little before you go off again."

"Sure, Mom," he said. I made some sandwiches, and we were out the door.

It was one of those perfect summer days New England is famous for. As we sat by the water taking in the golden sunlight, time seemed to stop. Todd's eyes were serene behind his wire-rimmed glasses as he told me about the things he hoped to learn and do in life.

Todd left for school later that afternoon with Rob, Scott, and me waving him off. Scott went over to a friend's for the night, and Rob and I had a quiet dinner. Stepping out back for a moment before bed, I watched a full moon rise into the clear New Hampshire night.

It was after midnight when the phone rang. The sound pulled me from a dark, disturbing dream. As I reached for the receiver, I knew that bad news was on the other end of the line.

"Mrs. Cruikshank?" It was a girl's voice, high and anxious. "I'm a friend of Todd's. I'm calling from the hospital in Dover. He's had an accident."

A nurse came on the line. "You need to come right away," she said. "Your son has suffered a bad fall."

As Rob and I raced down the highway, the moon seemed to accompany us, floating overhead. I remembered what my grandmother had told me. *God, I know you're up there. Please stay with Todd until I can get to him.*

At the hospital, a group of frightened students sat in the waiting room.

"What happened?" I asked.

"Todd said he was going to the roof to look at the moon. He must have slipped."

An image of Todd falling filled my mind. It was too terrible to bear. But when we were finally led in to see him, as he lay unconscious, his face was calm, almost tranquil. "He's suffered severe injuries," a doctor told us. "At this point I'm afraid there's very little we can do."

Shortly after dawn, Rob telephoned the house where Scott was staying, and an hour later he joined us at Todd's bedside. Just after noon on that August Saturday, Todd's heart monitor went flat. I squeezed his hand one last time. "I'll keep going, Todd," I found myself promising, "for your sake as much as for everyone else you've left behind."

Todd's funeral and the reception afterward were a minute-to-minute struggle. As soon as I could, I escaped to the bedroom. *Tomorrow is going to be another day without Todd,* I thought as I lay down. *And the day after that, and the day after that . . . God, how am I ever going to get through this?*

That night I had a strange dream. Looking down from above, I saw Rob and myself, asleep. In his room, Scott was asleep too. Then I saw Todd. He alone was awake, walking from room to room with his wire-rimmed glasses and that quiet, thoughtful look I knew so well.

I couldn't shake the feeling that the dream—so real, so vivid—was a message of some kind. I half expected another dream to come the following night, but none did. Then weeks later, I found myself tossing and turning in my bed. In the small hours of the morning, a migraine came on. At around six o'clock, I finally managed to drift off.

I dreamed I heard music. Someone was playing the piano. With a rush of joy, I recognized the tune: a piece I'd helped Todd learn for a recital, turning the pages for him as we sat side by side on our piano bench. "Aren't you bored just turning the pages?" he'd said.

"Never," I'd reassured him. "I love listening to you play." Now, as I listened to the notes of that long-forgotten piece, I felt as close to Todd as ever.

Waking next morning, I felt the same sense of reassurance I had after the first dream. But was I was simply creating these powerful images in an attempt to lessen my terrible sorrow? Maybe it was nothing more than that. . . .

Then came the third dream. I was standing in darkness, gazing up at the night sky. Every star in the universe seemed to be out. At the center of them all was the moon—full and beautiful, just like it was on the night Todd left us. I heard Todd's voice. He was so calm and happy, just like he had been on that last afternoon we spent together.

"Mom, when I fell, I wasn't frightened. It was like I was watching it all from above. I saw the ambulance arrive and my friends crying. But it was okay. God was with me. The only thing I couldn't face was the thought of your sadness."

After that dream, something changed in the way I looked at Todd's passing. There were still difficult days—and there still are, five years later. But because of what God showed me, I can keep the promise I made to Todd. The best way I can honor him is by continuing to find joy in life and to help others do so too.

When I find myself getting sad, I'll look up at the night sky and think again of my grandmother's words. "Even when we can't see the moon at all, it's still there in the heavens, looking over us." Just like the moon he loved so much, Todd's never far from us, either.

It is not the circumstances in which we are placed, but the spirit in which we face them, that constitutes our comfort.
—ELIZABETH T. KING

FACE THE DAWN

JENNY DENNIS

A stood in our living room and looked out the window at the rugged mountains beyond our small South African town, wondering what the future would bring. It was August 1989. A new government was coming into power in our country. The laws of apartheid were being challenged. A new day was dawning. "This is the future we've prayed for all these years," my husband, Alan, had said. It was hard to believe. All my life the only thing I'd known was the cruel system of racial segregation, as familiar and unyielding as the distant peaks. I was struggling to imagine life in South Africa without apartheid.

I heard Alan's car pull up. A few minutes later, he came inside. "Jenny, I've been offered a new parish," he said, then paused. "It's in Cape Town. The congregation is mostly white."

The plate I was carrying hit the floor with a smash. "I won't go, Alan," I said. Under apartheid, Alan and I were designated as "colored," or mixed race. I grew up in a suburb of Cape Town, one of the areas where colored people were permitted to live.

Yet before segregation was institutionalized, the people of South Africa had not lived so separately. My maternal grandmother was white, and she'd married my grandfather, whose parents were black and white; a similar situation existed on my father's side of the family. Growing up, I'd never have thought twice about the ranges

of complexion in my family except for the fact that adults had some mysterious rules about it. In school, light-skinned students were often given a "pencil test"—if a child's hair was thick enough to hold a pencil in place, he or she was declared colored and sent to separate schools. Even to a child, it was obvious schools for whites were better than ours. The ones for blacks were the worst.

One day my grandmother and I were taking the bus. We climbed the steep stairs to the colored section. She fell, hard. "Granny!" I cried. That's when the white riders turned away. They'd seen I was colored. "Someone help us," I pleaded. Finally some colored riders helped her up. Later, I told my grandmother I hated those white people. "No, Jenny," she said, taking me in her arms. "The only way to stop this evil is to love them. You must love." *Never*, I thought to myself, burying my face in her waist.

I met Alan at church. He too was colored, although lighter skinned than I. He was handsome, certainly, and charming. But most of all I admired his sense of hope for a better world and his belief that all people, no matter their "color," were essentially good, a view that deep in my heart I wasn't sure I could believe.

Alan went to seminary to be an Anglican priest. After his graduation we married. His first posting was to a large, wealthy church with a predominantly white congregation. I'd see whites at church functions and they would nod politely to me. On the street or in shops it was a different story. They walked past as if I didn't even exist.

Our daughter, Jill, was born in 1980, followed by Marc four years later. If anything, the apartheid system had grown harsher since my childhood. My children would have to learn to live under these laws, but I was determined that I would protect them as well.

Then came Jill's first ballet recital at age five. We left our excited little girl at the dressing room door and took our seats in the auditorium.

Onstage, Jill didn't dance with her usual joy. "She's probably just nervous," Alan said, patting my arm. Afterward, Jill asked, "Mommy and Daddy, why am I beige?" We asked her where she had gotten such an idea.

"I went to change in the dressing room with the other girls," Jill said. "A lady said, 'You're beige, you can't dress with the white children. Go to that colored bathroom down the hall.'" Jill started to cry. "The bathroom was dirty," she said.

I was so angry I could hardly speak. *God help me, I'll do whatever I must to protect my children from being hurt like this again.* When Alan moved on to congregations that were mixed or mostly colored, I felt much more comfortable. Like much of the South African clergy, black, colored and white, he became involved in peaceful protests against apartheid, often led by his archbishop, Desmond Tutu. Alan was arrested in church because he dared to air a video showing police brutality in our colored schools. In the dark of night, people would drive by our house shouting ugly threats or the phone would ring and someone with a thick Afrikaner accent would vow retribution against Alan and our children. It left a bitter taste in my mouth.

So standing in my living room that August day in 1989, as Alan told me about the offer to go to a primarily white congregation, I asked myself how I could put my painful experiences behind me and enter this brave new world that all South Africans were now stepping into as one people. Could I possibly set aside my own feelings of anger and distrust and be the wife of a pastor ministering to a white congregation? What about our children? "People don't change that fast," I said.

"We've got to move on, Jenny," Alan replied quietly. "We can't remain closed up in the old ways. We've got to build bridges for the future. We're no longer colored or black or white. We're all South Africans."

I knew my husband was right, yet a deep part of me resisted. There had been too much pain, too much hurt.

"Let's pray," I said to Alan. In my prayer I asked God to heal my wounds and give me the strength to love those I wanted to hate. The next day I agreed to drive with Alan past the new church. On the way, words came clearly to my mind, over and over: *Go, and the Lord said go.* At last I turned to Alan and said, "God wants us to go." *There,* I thought cautiously, *that's the first step.*

Alan was instituted as rector on February 11, 1990, at 3:00 P.M.—the exact hour that political leader Nelson Mandela was released from prison after twenty-seven years and made his historic freedom speech in Cape Town. "Our march to freedom is irreversible," he said. "I have cherished the ideal of a democratic and free society in which all persons live together in harmony and with equal opportunities." But as much as I wanted to believe that healing and reconciliation would come, I still couldn't quite accept it, not on the deep personal level where great healing begins, a level that every South African would have to reach if we were to ever have true reconciliation.

Our new congregation held a barbecue to welcome us. "How are you today, Mrs. Dennis," one parishioner greeted me. I wondered if he really was accepting me. I thought of those threatening voices I'd heard in the middle of the night and shuddered.

The congregation was wonderful, I couldn't deny it. At the sign of peace, people leaned across pews and crossed aisles to embrace. Yet I hung back even as my family joined in.

Women invited me over for tea or to go shopping. "No, thank you," I would always say, distrustful. At least I was polite enough to make an excuse.

It was a clear, warm day when we decided to go to the beach. Ten minutes from our house were the most beautiful beaches in Cape Town, beaches I'd only gazed at past signs that read "No coloreds or dogs allowed." Now there were no more signs. We pulled into the parking lot and started to unload the car. All at once a fearsome anxiety gripped me. "Are you sure it's all right for us to be here?" I asked.

Alan took my hand. Jill and Marc raced ahead of us, dying to get in the water. I stared around me. Everyone was white! *You're not supposed to be here.* Like tidal waves, first came uncertainty and then came fear, a fear that consumed me. I whirled and started back to the car, kicking up sand in my wake.

Alan and the children scrambled after me. "Jenny!" I looked over my shoulder. Alan's usually calm expression was determined. "Jenny, it was wrong that we had to suffer under the old ways, but things are changing. Don't you think it's time for you to change too?"

Jill had the same hurt look she'd had after the dance recital. But this time it was I who had hurt her. "Mommy, what's the matter?" Marc said, tears welling.

I stared at my children. I'd thought I was protecting them from the racism and pain that had poisoned my life. But were my own anger and inability to forgive just as damaging?

That night after the children were in bed, I got down on my knees. In a sickening rush, images flashed through my mind—the riders on the bus who wouldn't help my grandmother when they realized I was colored, the voices threatening my loved ones, the people who walked by as if I didn't exist. The memories made my throat tighten. *Lord, only you can deliver me from these terrible feelings. Help me find healing and reconciliation in your love. Help me become part of a world that is changing.*

All at once one memory came surging back, a memory of my grandmother holding me close and telling me, "You have to love, you have to love."

"But I hate them," I'd said to her.

"All hate does is come back to destroy you. When you love, your life keeps growing."

I stood up to find Alan beside me, his gaze steady and warm. He took me in his arms and I felt as if an enormous burden was beginning to lift.

The Lord's transformation of me was completed at church one Sunday morning. Alan planned to preach on grace and healing. "Jenny, would you like to be a part of it?" he asked. That morning, my hands shaking, I stood at the pulpit and looked out at the congregation I'd once wanted nothing to do with. "I didn't want to come to this church," I admitted. "I didn't want to deal with the rage and resentment I felt under the years of apartheid. But today I stand before you to thank you all for being an instrument of healing in my life. I know now that we can forgive and provide our children with the future they deserve and that God almighty means them to have."

I walked back to my pew. My cheeks were wet. Others all around were crying too. People rushed toward me, their arms open. This time I didn't pull away. This time I took a step forward, then another, into their embrace.

AUTHOR INDEX

TITLE INDEX

ACKNOWLEDGMENTS (continued from page 4)

JOHNSON, BARBARA. "I Thought I Had a Handle on Life, But Then It Fell Off" from *I'm So Glad You Told Me What I Didn't Wanna Hear.* Copyright © 1996 by Barbara Johnson. Word Publishing, Dallas. Used by permission of the author. KENNEDY, PAMELA. "A Father's Care," "Giving Thanks," and "Fear and Joy." Used by permission of the author. LAMOTT, ANNE. "Into Thin Mud" from *Traveling Mercies.* Copyright © 1999 by Anne Lamott. Used by permission of Pantheon Books, a division of Random House, Inc. NOUWEN, HENRI. "The Forward Look" from *Turn My Mourning into Dancing.* Copyright © 2001 by Henri Nouwen. Used by permission of W Publishing, Nashville, TN. PEALE, NORMAN VINCENT. "Nature's Resilience" from *Norman Vincent Peale's Treasury of Joy and Enthusiasm.* Published by Fleming Revell. Copyright © 1981 by the author. PEALE, RUTH STAFFORD. "The Gift of Adversity" from *A Lifetime of Positive Thinking.* Copyright © 2001 by Guideposts. REEVE, CHRISTOPHER. "The Lighthouse" from *Nothing Is Impossible.* Copyright © 2002 by Cambria Productions, Inc. Used by permission of Random House, Inc. REMEN RACHEL NAOMI. "Final Moments" from *Kitchen Table Wisdom.* Copyright © 1996 by Rachel Naomi Remen, M.D. Used by permission of Riverhead Books, an imprint of Penguin Group (USA) Inc. RUTLEDGE, ARCHIBALD. "Life's Extras" from *Peace in the Heart.* Copyright © 1927 by Archibald Rutledge. Used by permission of Doubleday, a division of Random House. RYBARIK, M. FRAN. "Michael's Gift." Used by permission of the author. SWINDOLL, LUCY. "Two Are Better Than One" from *We Brake for Joy!* by Barbara E. Johnson, Patsy Clairmont, Luci Swindoll, Sheila Walsh, Marilyn Meberg, Thelma Wells. Copyright © 1998 by Women of Faith, Inc. Used by permission of the Zondervan Corporation. TCHIVIDJIAN, GIGI GRAHAM. "Wise and Winsome" from *Footprints of a Pilgrim: The Life and Loves of Ruth Bell Graham.* Copyright © 2001 by Ruth Bell Graham. Used by permission of W Publishing, Nashville, TN. TREANOR, KATHLEEN. "Flowers of Compassion" and "Epiphany Among the Lilies" from *Ashley's Garden* by Kathleen Treanor with Candy Chand. Copyright © 2002 by the authors. Andrews McMeel Publishing. Used by permission of Peter Rubie Literary Agency for the authors. WHITE, JEANNE. An excerpt from *Weeding Out the Tears* by Jeanne White with Susan Dworkin. Copyright © 1997 by Jeanne White. Published by Avon Books. Used by permission of the Stuart Krichevsky Literary Agency, Inc. WHITESTONE, HEATHER. "Don't Second-Guess God" from *Listening With My Heart.* Copyright © 1997 by Heather Whitestone. Used by permission of Doubleday, a division of Random House, Inc. Our sincere thanks to A. J. CRONIN for "The Turning Point of My Life" and ALAN DEVOE for "Wise Animals I Have Known," from *Norman Vincent Peale's Treasury of Joy and Enthusiasm.* Previously published in *Readers' Digest.*

All other stories from *Angels on Earth,* copyright © Guideposts, Carmel, NY, and *Guideposts* magazine, copyright © Guideposts, Carmel, NY.

All possible care has been taken to fully acknowledge the ownership and use of the selections in this book. If any mistakes or omissions have occurred, they will be corrected in subsequent editions, provided notification is sent to the publisher.

Embracing Joy

I asked, "How many of you have heard of Helen Keller?" and out of five hundred students only three or four raised their hands.

They had no role models! I was nearly speechless with surprise. Since surrendering my title, I have been involved with the Helen Keller Eye Research Foundation of Birmingham, Alabama, and I believe all deaf and blind people should be acquainted with her story. Later during that trip I spoke in a public high school for hearing girls, and when I asked how many had heard of Helen Keller, nearly every girl raised her hand. Why didn't the deaf students—who desperately needed her example—know about Helen Keller?

Just thinking about that oversight made my heart race. Helen Keller had been my role model my entire life, her example had given me hope. So many of her inspiring quotes had encouraged me to strive for my dreams.

I soon began to understand why none of the deaf Taiwanese students had heard of Helen Keller. They are still living in an age that considers deafness nearly as great an obstacle to learning as mental retardation; they couldn't seem to stop marveling over the fact that I was a living, thinking, rational human being. During one question-and-answer session a high school girl stood up and asked, "Do you think you will have a normal marriage?"

Nonplussed, I answered, "My husband looks at me as a person, not as a disability."

To their credit, many people in Taiwan are striving to change things. I met one mother, Joanna Nichols, who had gone to the United States to learn about education for deaf people. Taking responsibility for her deaf daughter's education, she has studied cued speech, acoupedics, sign language, and oral speech. She is trying to make a difference not only for her daughter but for all deaf children. With the help of Citibank, she was instrumental in arranging my visit to Taiwan.

Many parents with deaf children today have high expectations for them. I am concerned that parents who see or hear me may think their children capable of immediate speech. I want to give parents hope, but that hope should be tempered with realism. I did not speak very well when I was little. It took me six years to learn how to say my last name correctly. In language skills I have always lagged far behind my age level.

I hope parents will not expect their deaf children to speak well and use perfect English grammar when they are young. Maturity will bring progress, and your hard work will bring results. Just don't expect too much too soon. Enjoy every moment with your children because life is short. God has not given you this precious child in order to put you to work twenty-four hours a day. God has given you this deaf child because he or she needs your love. Children hunger for love more than success.

One quote has never lost its power to move me: "Some people complain because God put thorns on roses, while others praise him for putting roses among thorns." How true that is! We must learn to recognize and praise God for the good things he has brought into our lives.

That was the message I took to the people of Taiwan. They were lovely; no one could be more generous or gracious. The girls in the public high school brought me flowers and a teddy bear, and they were eager to practice their English with me. I felt so much respect, love, and warm kindness. They wanted to hear my speech, they wanted to know about my then-fiancé, they wanted to know about being Miss America. One girl, however, stumped me with her question. She asked: "If you could hear for one day, what would you do?"

I was caught unprepared, so on the spur of the moment I replied that I'd probably try to hear as many unfamiliar words as I could, because it's hard to use new vocabulary correctly when you can't hear them being pronounced.

But today, if asked the same question, I'd probably reply that I'd spend the day on the beach with John, just listening to his precious voice. Matters of the heart are now more precious to me than matters of the mind.

Life is a journey, and God directs the person who asks for his help . . . and follows his dream. He allowed me to become deaf, and I'm grateful for his wisdom. Being deaf taught me to be disciplined, and then my heart taught me to dance.

If I hadn't learned discipline and dance, I would never have entered a pageant . . . and won.

If I hadn't been Miss America, I would never have met John. Neither would I be writing this book.

I can't second-guess God. If I could be anyone I wanted to be, I would be Heather Whitestone McCallum. I'm happy being who God called me to be. I still have dreams—I'd love to learn ice dancing, and I'd love to dance more regularly—but my life belongs to God. I'll follow where he leads.

*The pessimist sees the difficulty in every opportunity;
the optimist sees the opportunity in every difficulty.*

—L. P. JACKS

ONE DOOR AT A TIME

SHELLY BRADY

When my husband, John, and I had our first child twenty years ago, we agreed I'd be a stay-at-home mom. That meant we'd have to make do on a single income. We scrimped and saved so we could keep up with the mortgage and our student loans. We ate a lot of macaroni-and-cheese dinners. We didn't even go to the movies anymore.

I clipped coupons and tracked down sales. Tuesday was when the thrift stores put out their "new" merchandise. Wednesday was when the meat and dairy section goods were marked at half price just prior to their expiration date. Saturday morning meant getting to the garage sales before anyone else. But none of this was unfamiliar. I grew up wanting. So I had set my sights on realistic goals that would get me out of poverty: a college education, a solid marriage, and a career. I'd done it all, yet I still couldn't imagine things would ever really go right for me. My faith felt more like a safety net than a reason to have hope for a better life.

Things took a turn one day when I got a phone call. "Shelly? This is Bill Porter," the voice on the end of the line said. Bill was a door-to-door salesman I'd delivered packages for in high school. "Would you be interested in coming back a couple of days a week to fill orders for me?" I talked about it with John, and then went to work for Bill.

The first thing you notice about Bill is his unusual appearance. His ears are very large. He walks—or rather, shuffles—stooped over. His right hand is balled up almost into a fist. And he takes a long time to get his words out. When I was a teen I was too shy to ask about it. But one day after I started working for him again I posed the question.

"Bill, do you have MS or something like that?" I asked.

"I have cerebral palsy," he answered matter-of-factly. I think he knew I was nervous talking about it.

"But . . . what does that mean? How did you get it? Will it get worse?"

"The doctor's forceps damaged my brain at birth. My condition will never get any worse. But it won't get any better, either. It doesn't stop me from accomplishing whatever I set my mind to."

Bill's optimism amazed me, especially in contrast to my own tendency toward pessimism. He gave credit to his parents, who taught him a strong faith. They fought to get him into public school, and after he graduated his father told him, "Get a job." He wasn't being harsh. It's just that they'd never coddled Bill; instead, they'd always insisted he could do anything he set his mind to, and they never let him give up.

Bill got an interview with Watkins, Incorporated, a company whose salesmen peddle home remedies and spices door to door. Bill told the director, "Selling is in my blood. It almost doesn't matter what the product is, as long as I believe in it. Give me a chance and you'll see."

The director gave Bill a job—on a trial basis. He knocked on door after door and heard no after no. Then Bill started making sales. He walked his route eight hours a day, or more, and became the company's top salesman in the entire Northwest.

It wasn't easy. Every morning Bill's alarm went off at 4:45 A.M. His bus downtown left at 7:20 A.M. Bill needed all that time because he doesn't like to dress in a rush. "Appearance is essential," he said. Each morning he put on clean socks, pressed trousers, and a fresh white shirt. He'd leave his cuffs unbuttoned, his wing tips loosely tied, and his tie in his briefcase. Some friends at a hotel near where he made a bus transfer attended to those loose ends. Bill would hit the streets, knocking on every single door, telling himself, "The next customer will say yes." The key is, Bill believes they'll all say yes eventually.

I kept working for Bill, even after I had a few more children. John was making more money, but I continued to scrimp and save. Honestly, it had become a compulsion. I still went through life with a sense of foreboding. Faith was still an insurance policy against disaster rather than a way to meet life head-on. Bill used his faith every day, getting out of bed and expecting the best. Would I ever look at life that way?

Even my husband was frustrated with me. One weekend John wanted to go to a movie. "We can catch the seven o'clock show."

"Honey, can't we go to the matinee?" I asked. "It's cheaper."

"We can afford it."

He was right, but I couldn't stop worrying about money and the future. It all stemmed from my childhood, and I'd never be able to overcome that.

One winter day a storm was forecast. To Bill the weather report was good news. "Perfect for a door-to-door salesman," he said. "Everyone's home!" So he bundled up and made his rounds until he'd made his quota. By then, the buses had stopped running because the roads were so bad. He had to hitchhike home, only to discover the steep driveway leading to his front door was a sheet of ice. He tried to get up it again and again, but kept falling down. Finally he got down on his hands and knees and crawled to the front door, thoroughly satisfied with his day's work. He told me about it the next morning. It was as if the cumulative effect of working with Bill and his optimism sank in. I wanted to stop worrying about life and start enjoying it.

It's been twenty years now that I've worked for Bill. Once in a while those old worries start in on me. It's then that I think about my friend Bill crawling up his icy driveway. I hear him saying, "There are no obstacles, Shelly. Only challenges." When I follow his example, I'm able to let go and feel free.

Yes, Bill Porter's finally got me looking forward to the opportunities God opens for us, one door at a time.

And these days, when my family goes to the movies we see the full-priced show—and splurge on popcorn.

*You may accept the inevitable with bitterness
and resentment or with patience and grace.*
—PAUL BRUNTON

GIVING THANKS

PAMELA KENNEDY

A yanked the rake through the leaves with angry strokes, sending dust and sticks flying. Stopping for a moment, I looked around the yard to assess my progress. When we purchased the house, I had loved the shade offered by the towering oaks and maples. How could I have forgotten that sooner or later those leaves would fall in abundance on our spacious lawn? But it was more than the chore of raking that fed my anger. I had received word that a friend was struggling with a serious illness, and I was angry about the unfairness of suffering. My husband had been called away on a business trip, and I was angry about being left alone. As I meditated on my anger, it grew until I took it out by flailing away at the leaves covering my yard. I needed a break. Maybe a cup of coffee would restore my spirits.

As I relaxed in the kitchen with my coffee, my glance fell on the picture on the refrigerator that my granddaughter had drawn in her Sunday school class. The primitive crayon drawing depicted a scraggly cat sitting on a table. On the floor next to the table was a broken vase, several long-stemmed flowers, and a blue blob I interpreted to be spilled water. Someone had written in neat printing across the bottom of the page: In every thing give thanks.

I almost laughed out loud. Give thanks for a yard full of leaves and no one to help me? Give thanks for a friend with a life-threatening illness? And then I looked at the paper again, realizing something that I had missed the first time I read it.

The word was *in*, not *for*.

I sipped my coffee slowly, meditating on the words under the scraggly cat. Could I find a reason for thanks *in* all these circumstances, if not *for* them? I looked out the window at the towering oaks, now filled with bare branches instead of fluttering leaves. A gray squirrel scampered across a limb and into the safety of his snug nest. "Thank you Lord," I whispered, "for the way you care for all your creatures, great and small." I thought of my dear friend and all the memories we shared; then I whispered a prayer of thanks for her kind and gentle friendship, her sweet example of courage. I smiled recalling the phone conversation I had that morning with my husband and thanked God for such a loving companion. Then my glance rested again on the drawing of the cat, and I was thankful that my children were raising their own children with care and integrity. By the time I had finished the coffee, my anger was gone, dissipated like the steam rising from the teakettle.

With renewed energy, I pulled on my boots and gloves and buttoned my work jacket. Grabbing the rake, I headed for the pile of leaves I had left only a half hour earlier. Somehow the day seemed brighter, the task easier, the wind less threatening. Raising my face to the sky, I thanked God that in the midst of my selfishness, he had spoken his truth and taught me the liberating secret of giving thanks in all things.